Explore the startling, behind-the-scenes facts:

- Hamilton Jordan's secret negotiations.
- Ayatollah Khomeini and his phenomenal rise to power.
- The truth about America's alleged crimes in Iran. Did Washington really betray the Shah, and what was the mysterious role of General Huyser in the last days of the Shah's regime?
- The U.N. Special Commission.

THE IRAN CRISIS

by
Doug Wead

haven books
A division of Logos International
Plainfield, N.J. 07060

THE IRAN CRISIS
Copyright © 1980 by Logos International
All rights reserved
Printed in the United States of America
Library of Congress Catalog Card Number: 80-81064
International Standard Book Number: 0-88270-433-3
Logos International, Plainfield, New Jersey 07060

To Shannon Douglas Wead,
whose integrity and strength of will
have been an inspiration to me.

Acknowledgments

The author would like to thank numerous unnamed sources in Iran, Canada, and the United States who risked their reputations, careers, and sometimes their lives to provide critical information on the fast-moving events.

Special thanks to Mary Gordon Achor, Darryl Hicks, Keith Kunzler, and my wife, Gloria, for providing treatments of some chapters and editorial assistance. Mrs. Helen Langston of the Springfield, Missouri, library was especially helpful in emergency situations.

Publisher's Preface

When the crisis in Iran became front-page news, my curiosity about this country in the Middle East was aroused. I immediately turned to various maps of the area; when I compared the historical maps with current ones, I realized that the nation we now know as Iran is the same country as the ancient biblical land of Persia.

Because my given name is Daniel I have always had a strong fascination about the ancient prophet Daniel. I turned to the Scriptures to see what I could discover about Iran from the book of Daniel. It was interesting to learn that Daniel was assigned to be first president to help govern the Kingdom of Media under Darius, the king.

Darius was assisted by his nephew, Cyrus, in conquering Asia Minor. For this reason, in

THE IRAN CRISIS

536 BC Cyrus inherited the crowns of Persia and Media; he then united these kingdoms into the Medo-Persian Empire. The prophet Isaiah had foreseen that Cyrus would be the deliverer and restorer of Judah.

It was Cyrus, King of Persia, who commanded those who had been part of Israel to return to their land to rebuild Solomon's Temple. He proceeded to return all the gold and silver vessels which had been taken from the Temple in Jerusalem.

Throughout its history, Iran had practiced benevolence toward the Israelites. This was true under the Shah as well, but the Ayatollah Khomeini has taken an opposite stand by publicly expressing contempt for Israel.

This issue and several related questions troubled me. Is the present world focus on Iran more than an accident? Will Iran fulfill the prophetic legends of Ezekiel and be a prominent participant in the great Armageddon? What events led up to the present crisis?

Because I believe the world wants answers to these questions and related ones, I commissioned Doug Wead to research the issues and provide us with factual information in *The Iran Crisis*. Doug is author of the best-selling *People's Temple—People's Tomb* and nine other books. He is an accomplished writer and

Publisher's Preface

researcher. In fact, Doug is better qualified than most writers to prepare a book on this topic because he has been to Iran many times, and knows the culture, people, religion and political systems of this strategic region in a personal way.

The first-hand research for this book has taken Doug thousands of miles; he has succeeded in obtaining behind-the-scenes information in his effort to unravel the mysteries surrounding the hostage dilemma. As you will discover, *The Iran Crisis* reads like a suspenseful novel with elements of international intrigue and espionage. It is easy to understand, and Doug presents objective facts to enable you to draw conclusions for yourself. It is investigative journalism at its best. You will see that the events in Iran go beyond the newspaper reports. Doug Wead has eradicated much of the mystery, giving us vital information and a prelude to the inevitable events of the future.

Dan Malachuk

Contents

Acknowledgments **vi**
Publisher's Preface **vii**

1. The Embassy Takeover **13**
2. The Shah **31**
3. The White Revolution **55**
4. The Rise of Khomeini **71**
5. Showdown with Carter **89**
6. Islam Aflame **103**
7. The Missing Hostages **119**
8. The Invasion of Afghanistan **137**
9. The Canadian Caper **155**
10. Return of Bani-Sadr **169**
11. The U.N. Commission **187**

Appendixes:

A—Code of Conduct for the Shah's Family **207**

B—Mohammed Pahlavi's Farewell Speech **211**

C—President Carter's State of the Union Address **213**

1

The Embassy Takeover

He looked like a wizard out of a Tolkien fantasy. He had bushy eyebrows and a huge, gray beard. His exterior was calm, even sleepy, and yet a mysterious energy emanated from some deep reservoir within. One imagined that the seventy-nine-year-old Ayatollah Khomeini could bring thunder and lightning with the feeble wave of his ancient hand.

It was Sunday morning, November 4, 1979, in the quiet and holy city of Qum. The street was packed with young people jostling for a glimpse of Khomeini. Inside the old mullah's humble residence, advisers hummed and buzzed around while the Ayatollah himself sat perfectly still, a calm figure in the midst of the moving hive. The only sign of life in him was the opening and closing of his eyelids very, very slowly

THE IRAN CRISIS

expressing his boredom and contempt for the excitement his presence created.

The Ayatollah was angry today and the audience could sense his righteous indignation. That mysterious energy seemed dangerously close to the surface. The revolution is under heavy attack, he complained. The words were carefully passed along, one by one, like delicate pieces of china, even reaching the crowds outside. One student was told that the American embassy is the center of intrigue. He had tough words for the British, too, the old mullah still erroneously believing the United Kingdom had given sanctuary to Shahpour Bakhtiar, the Shah's last prime minister. But, strangely, he kept returning to the American embassy, not Carter whom he had recently labeled "the great Satan," not the CIA, not the Shah, not Americans in general, but the embassy in particular, that "nest of spies" in Tehran.

Eighty miles to the north, in Tehran itself, young people demonstrated outside the American embassy on Taleghani Street. It was not one of the giant mobs that often filled Western television screens. Just a few hundred students and unemployed youths, a demonstration far less ominous than Khomeini's comments, which, though whispered, had sounded like thunder.

The Embassy Takeover

By mid-morning, some of the Tehran demonstrators were joined by leftist students, but the huge walls of the American embassy appeared unimpressed. The whole event smacked of spontaneity; none of the spectators nearby suspected violence. The crowd swelled to close to five hundred, but buses and automobiles continued to race by, some curious pedestrians paused to look for a moment. Others, without breaking stride, craned their necks to take in as much of the scene as they could before passing from view. Street vendors, preparing pistachio nuts, did not even look up.

When Khomeini's words reached the embassy, the demonstrators' mood shifted quickly. Dozens of guns began to appear. As if being directed by some spiritual magic issuing from Qum eighty miles away, the students found a pair of steel shears. The chains holding together the giant iron gates of the U.S. embassy popped open and the crowd poured into the compound. It was 11:00 A.M.

It had happened so quickly and easily; it was so low-key by Iranian standards, that even many of the demonstrators were stunned. Only the week before, an Iranian newspaper had commented on the love-hate relationship between Persia and America. One day the embassy

THE IRAN CRISIS

is mobbed by Iranians seeking visas to the West, the next day by crowds shouting, "Death to America." Now curious youths scampered over the walls, dropping into the twenty-seven-acre compound. More guns were passed around, bullhorns began to appear, and news of the break-in at the embassy spread through the streets. A huge mob began to form outside where self-appointed student cheerleaders shouted enthusiastically and rehearsed the onlookers with chants, "Death to the Shah!" "Death to Carter!"

The students inside secured the unoccupied Ambassador's residence and turned to face the chancellery. "Fort Apache," as the American embassy employees call it, is a two-story brick building with armor plating and plenty of grillwork. Young Iranians, flushed with a sense of their own success and power, shouted up at the monster.

The Americans inside were making desperate attempts to get help. Leftist guerrillas had broken into the compound that very February, only two weeks after the Ayatollah had returned to the jubilant Iranian masses. William Sullivan and one hundred American personnel had been held hostage then, but Khomeini's makeshift Revolutionary Army had defeated the guerrillas and freed the hostages within a couple of hours.

The Embassy Takeover

Sullivan was gone now and the stubborn Khomeini government had refused a new American ambassador. That had left L. Bruce Laingen, U.S. chargé d'affaires, as the senior embassy official, but, as students mounted their takeover on November 4, Laingen was not there. An American political officer closeted himself in the vacant ambassador's office, finally reaching the U.S. chargé d'affaires by telephone. Laingen was at the Iranian Foreign Ministry, seemingly a stroke of luck. Without breaking his telephone connection, the head of the United States' delegation in Iran pleaded for the Revolutionary militia to be called in to protect the embassy.

At noon, the mob on Taleghani Street grew. Student demonstrators inside suddenly relocked the embassy gates. This was their demonstration and the Americans they had bagged were theirs too. The Iranian people could watch and cheer them on from the streets.

For a while, "Fort Apache" appeared invincible. Most of the students paused before her, momentarily puzzled about how to break in. Others methodically went about their work, apparently well prepared for the operation.

While an elite group worked their way into the last fortress on the compound, five others hauled out a captured American flag, stood on the embassy ramparts and lifted it high into the sky. The mobs outside shouted thunderously, "Death to America!" The chant shook the ground beneath the mighty chancellery. The American flag was set aflame and tossed into the gray sky.

The Americans kept their pipeline to Laingen and the outside world, but nothing could be confirmed. Laingen, maintaining his station at the Foreign Ministry, pleaded urgently but Khomeini's government seemed maddeningly cumbersome and slow in response. Officials in the Iranian Foreign Ministry offered sympathy, "The militia would surely be sent in."

At the embassy, marines inside Fort Apache moved to full combat positions. All employees were herded to the top floor, the most secure sanctuary in the chancellery. Below them, Iranians had finally breached the building and were now coughing their way along the tear-gas trail that led to the entrapped Americans.

Even with students outside the sanctuary, Laingen wouldn't relay the "final destruction" order. Did the Iranian government understand the consequences of what was happening? Laingen received word that the consulate section of the compound had also been breached. The U.S. government had just spent a half

The Embassy Takeover

million dollars to rebuild it.

At 12:52 P.M., Laingen reluctantly gave the order to the Americans in the embassy, "Final destruction." The Americans began feeding classified documents into the shredders and one security incinerator. They held the students off until 3:30 P.M., when a marine opened the door and the Iranians rushed in.

The large mobs on the streets waited patiently. Breathless, newsmen began arriving at the scene. One, with a British accent, shouted repeatedly through the gates, "Are you going to burn it?" The American Broadcasting Company made an immediate decision to dispatch a crew to Tehran. The other American television networks hesitated, giving their rival a several-day advantage to scoop the story.

Within the hour, a coalition of student leaders returned to the main entrance. "We are the Muslim students of the Imam Khomeini Line," they said. They issued Communiqué Number One, denouncing the United States for protecting the criminal Shah, "responsible for the deaths of thousands of Iranians."

Appearing in single file behind them were some of the American embassy employees. They were blindfolded and bound tightly. Other students pulled and jostled them to the gates, presenting them to the shouting mob.

THE IRAN CRISIS

The roar was overpowering. They had been rehearsed for almost an hour; now they responded with a superb performance, louder and in more perfect unison than ever. "Death to the Shah!" "Death to America!" The now numerous and rival self-appointed cheerleaders stood on embassy walls or on nearby roofs exhorting the crowds with great seriousness, as if, without their sweat and hand wrenching, the mob would not have peeped. But the most important message came from the militant student leaders, speaking without microphones to journalists standing near the embassy gates. "Give us the Shah," they said, "and we will release the American spies!"

The President of the United States was at Camp David when the news of Iran reached him. He was on the phone instantly to his foreign affairs adviser and secretary of state. The National Security Council began a marathon emergency session.

The news media's initial reaction to the embassy takeover was quite cynical. Presidential politics had just pushed the Cambodian famine off the front pages. Ted Kennedy was on his way to trouncing an incumbent president. That very week, national news magazines spoke of a "crisis in leadership." Ten Republican contend-

The Embassy Takeover

ers had jumped into the fray to challenge their party's front-runner, Ronald Reagan. The presidency appeared to be up for grabs. The events in Iran struck many as another nail in the political coffin of Jimmy Carter.

Indeed, Iran was said to be a graphic illustration of a confusing and contradictory foreign policy which lacked a grand design and which was courting international disaster. When the Shah was in control and an ally, Carter's support was said to be halfhearted, as if the Shah's fall would not be a bad idea. Now, with the Shah in exile and a new fragile Khomeini government in power, a government warning us urgently that their nation would be torn asunder by domestic discord if we gave the Shah sanctuary, we suddenly opened our arms to him.

The consensus in Washington was that Carter had better get out of this one in a hurry if he wanted to hang on to his slim chance at reelection. The other candidates grandly promised to refrain from debating the crisis. The President should have complete freedom to resolve the issue, but at least one admitted privately there was not much he could do.

There was some ambivalent news on Monday. Iran's Prime Minister Mehdi Bazargan promised help in getting the hostages released, but for weeks Washington had been getting signals that the Bazargan government was tottering. It appeared that the seventy-nine-year-old Ayatollah would make the decision about this situation and indications were very clear that his mind had not yet been made up. Seyyed Ahmed Khomeini, the Ayatollah's son, visited the embassy that Monday morning and emerged from discussions with student militants with the startling announcement that he, like his father, supported the takeover.

Washington was shaken. Was Ahmed really speaking for his father? Would Khomeini approve the taking of hostages? And, more importantly, why was the administration so uninformed of the apparent weakness of the Khomeini-appointed Bazargan government? Who was running Iran?

Monday evening, the Ayatollah Khomeini lashed out at the United Kingdom. The British government was commanded to return Shahpour Bakhtiar, the Shah's last prime minister. Students stormed into the British embassy but, after six hours, the takeover was abandoned. Word had spread that the old Ayatollah was mistaken. The British had not given sanctuary to Bakhtiar. The Shah's last prime minister was in France, where the Ayatollah Khomeini himself had taken refuge. The situation on the

The Embassy Takeover

streets of Tehran was confusing and unpredictably dangerous.

Tuesday, November 6, 1979. It was now clear that Khomeini backed the embassy takeover. The Bazargan government resigned. The first prime minister of the revolution was understandably bitter. Weeks earlier he had told a television audience that the "government was a knife without a blade." Students on the street shouted that Bazargan was a "traitor," and so, the man who had languished for years in the Shah's prison, Khomeini's own choice for prime minister, was now being advised by friends to flee the country.

Khomeini's personally appointed, fifteen-man Revolutionary Council now officially took the reins of government. Huge pictures of the Ayatollah began to appear among the mobs in the street. On this Tuesday, a divided and complex Iran appeared united behind the mystical and angry old mullah who openly sneered at the most powerful nation on earth. The people in the streets expressed no fear of American retaliation; rather there was great excitement and Islamic pride. The American giant appeared to be bound tightly, held in place by the moral authority and righteousness of one man.

In the West, observers were beginning to

appreciate how complicated the situation had become. Khomeini was taking a public position from which he could not easily back down.

It had been a bold decision, so some in the West reasoned. It was apparently motivated by the domestic political situation. The Revolutionary militia was even now battling Kurdish armies seeking autonomy for their province in northwestern Iran. Hundreds had already died in battle. Oil workers in Khuzestan were chafing under the continual interference by Muslim religious leaders. The ayatollahs had forced one oil administrator out of office and had even tried to arrest him for speaking out publicly. A few weeks before the takeover, large mobs of women had taken to the streets to demonstrate against Khomeini's chauvinistic legalism. The Iranian economy was faltering, some food items were scarce. The vaunted Persian Air Force was grounded for lack of parts. Persistent problems with neighboring Iraq threatened to break into open warfare. The clever old mullah was acting out of an instinct for survival, the rationale went. He was a ruthless, self-righteous legalist, this old Ayatollah, but, in a crude, instinctive sense, he was a born politician. Rouse the people against the American devils and they will forget their own sectarian interests and be distracted from the

The Embassy Takeover

country's economic woes.

Still, there were some in the State Department who were beginning to doubt that Khomeini was so clever. Admittedly, the Ayatollah appeared to be exploiting his reborn popularity. A new constitution was being drafted and rushed to a vote. But information coming from Iran suggested they were dealing with an unstable, extremely bitter and very uninformed old man. When a recent interviewer had pressed the Ayatollah about his ban on Western music, the astonishing fact slipped out that he had never even heard of Beethoven or Bach, let alone the Beatles. It was becoming apparent in Washington that the provincial, religious leader was appallingly ignorant of anything but Islamic tradition and, thus, normal diplomatic signals as well as international law were beyond his grasp.

By Wednesday, the Carter administration announced it had ruled out a military response. Nothing would be done to jeopardize the hostages. The United States would seek a peaceful solution to the problem. There was some grumbling among a few congressmen.

Americans, shocked and outraged by their apparent helplessness, could not help but wonder how the Israelis would have responded to such terrorism. Calls for an Entebbe-style raid were flying around Washington. Some

THE IRAN CRISIS

Republicans were privately reminding each other of Gerald Ford and his successful handling of the Mayaguez incident. We could, at least, have kept the military option publicly open, a congressman argued. "You don't announce to your enemy that whatever he does, you won't fight him anyway." A political cartoon appeared showing a ghostly John Wayne, armed to the teeth, galloping towards Iran, to the rescue of his countrymen.

But most members of government and most members of the press paused and considered Carter's decision. It was a chess move which looked better the longer one studied it. The Iranian situation was not one which lent itself to the style of an Entebbe or Mayaguez anyway. Even the military joined in agreement.

Additionally, the announcement of "no military response" was having a curious effect on world public opinion. There were stirrings of genuine sympathy for America and respect for her cautiousness and reluctance to use power. Diplomatic missions had to be respected. Terrorism could disrupt normal communications between states. The United Nations seemed especially sensitive to what had happened and, therefore, susceptible to a U.S. effort to use its authority to secure the release of the hostages.

Finally, in post-Vietnam America, Carter's

The Embassy Takeover

promise seemed to check in place forces which might be aroused by anything smacking of military adventurism. But, if America was to remain patient with Carter's decision to rule out the military, it would depend on the success of his "peaceful means" of obtaining the hostages' release.

The first diplomatic effort was to dispatch Lyndon Johnson's former Attorney General, Ramsey Clark, and an ex-State Department officer, William Miller, to Tehran. Miller was on record as an opponent of America's pro-Shah stance, and Ramsey Clark had been positively ecstatic over the Ayatollah. Clark had visited with Khomeini during his time of exile in France and was even then a supporter. The two men would be Carter's personal emissaries to the Ayatollah.

Washington also took up a surprising offer by the Palestine Liberation Organization. The P.L.O., popular with the new Iranian Revolutionary government, suggested they try their hand at mediation. It was a delicate game, America juggling its promise to Israel not to recognize the P.L.O., with the realities of a crisis demanding flexibility.

Many applauded the U.S. State Department in this crisis hour. Their tactical skills were so varied and resourceful that the country forgot the charges that an uncertain, confusing foreign policy strategy had landed it in trouble in the first place.

Ironically, with each diplomatic failure, the Carter administration appeared to be even more successful in its handling of the affair. The Clark-Miller delegation failed. The Ayatollah would not receive any American devils, even these who had supported him. The P.L.O. emissaries failed, retreating from Tehran with some embarrassment, fearful that their propaganda triumph had only further isolated Iran. Pakistan's efforts failed. A Vatican envoy got further than most. The Ayatollah would speak with Pro Nuncio Annibalo Bugnini, since he was a religious leader, but the Pope's representative was told the same story: when the United States returns the Shah for trial, the hostages will be released. Yet, as each mission failed, America looked more responsible and compassionate. The Ayatollah was thought to be drifting further out to sea on a block of melting ice.

America was openly surprised at her unity in this moment of insult and blackmail. It was as if she were awakening from a bad dream, the division and bitterness of the Vietnam years behind her. A surge of nationalism broke across the country. Bells rang, flags appeared, Iranian student marches were broken up by angry, arm-

The Embassy Takeover

swinging patriotic fanatics. With the nation temporarily galvanized behind him, the President and his State Department slowly plotted their escalation of pressure on the Revolutionary government of Iran.

Meanwhile, Wednesday evening in the ancient, holy city of Qum, with its thirteenth-century Muslim mosques rising as giant black silhouettes against the nighttime sky, the Ayatollah Khomeini and his advisers met in the old mullah's living room. A single, bare light bulb swung from the ceiling. Outside, small armed bands of the Revolutionary militia strolled the darkened, dusty street. A half dozen reporters waited behind a barricade at the end of the block.

It had sounded like a simple proposition. "Return the Shah and we will return your spies!" Now Iran was finding itself increasingly isolated. Egyptian President Anwar Sadat had called the events a "disgrace to Islam." The Ayatollah's international image was in transition. If this was a Tolkien wizard, it was no Gandalf, but rather a Saruman, grown sour and evil. The energy which seemed just beneath the surface of the mullah was no longer perceived as moral authority or the charisma of the self-disciplined, but rather it was seen as pure hatred. A very bitter, determined hatred purposely beamed to a single individual—beamed to an individual as modern and international as the Ayatollah was traditional and provincial. They held very little in common, this old mullah and the subject of his hatred—only their pride, their stubbornness, and their ruthlessness.

It was a man dying of cancer the Ayatollah hated. A man lying in his bed on the seventeenth floor of the Sloan-Kettering Cancer Center in New York City. He was an international criminal, the old Muslim mullah said. The hostages would die, the world could go to hell, but the seventy-nine-year-old Ayatollah Ruhollah Khomeini would have his revenge.

The only word released from Qum that night was that the Imam had retired for a long weekend. The world would have to wait till Monday.

2

The Shah

The Shah of Iran, dying of cancer at the Sloan-Kettering Center in New York City, had a reputation for being a survivor. Even in childhood, there was a mystique about his destiny. He was the prince of a storybook; the plot was predetermined, the script already written. Nothing could stop it from unfolding. Pahlavi family lore abounded with tales of the youth emerging unscathed from a riding accident or surviving typhoid. Indeed, Mohammed Pahlavi bragged repeatedly that he was under God's protection and could not be harmed.

For an entire generation, the Shah of Iran had wrestled with Russian, British and American intrigue, surviving numerous threats to his rule and even plots on his life. On one occasion, his would-be assassin leaped from the crowd, firing a pistol three times. The Persian monarch spun around, blood streaming from his neck and face, while courtiers and spectators dove for cover. The man began firing again, the Shah now out in the open, alone, twisting and ducking. Blood began spurting from the king's shoulder and then, unexpectedly, the assailant's gun jammed. The Shah of Iran pulled himself up, proud and dignified, a lion staring contemptuously at the flea who had just attacked. The legend continued to build, year after year—Mohammed Pahlavi was a survivor.

So it was not paranoia that caused the aging Ayatollah Khomeini to fear the deposed and exiled monarch. Mohammed Pahlavi had fallen from power before and been placed back on the Peacock Throne by the very Americans who now so generously granted him asylum. The mullahs in Qum may have concluded that the Shah, indeed the entire Pahlavi family, must die, and with them, all treaties, all strings leading to foreign governments. Only then would the Islamic Revolution be safe and only then could it hope to return Persia to its authentic Muslim roots.

Mohammed Reza Pahlavi was not the first Shah of Iran. In the nineteenth century, a whole series of them ruled from the capital city.

The Shah

These were not feudal Bedouin chieftains galloping across the sands on their dromedaries with Saracen knives gripped between their teeth. These kings were addicted to luxuries, their palaces filled with silken pillows and gold. Even then, the shahs seemed to look westward, spending their time negotiating business and pleasure in the parlors of Europe.

Persia was fair game for exploitation then. Autonomous mountain tribes and Bedouin bands of outlaws roamed the countryside. The corrupt shahs of the Qajar dynasty seldom ruled beyond Tehran and its immediate surroundings, but their exploitation of the whole country via British, Russian, or Ottoman troops was extensive.

Twenty-five years of future customs' income were sold to the British for a pittance in order to finance the immediate pleasures of one Qajar shah. When this shah was assassinated, the new monarch sold his nation's oil rights to Great Britian for forty thousand dollars. The Russians were given control of the tobacco-opium trade; the railroads went to the British.

By the twentieth century, Persia was at the breaking point. Russian and British troops occupied huge slices of the country. Sectarian wars broke out across the mountains and deserts. Tehran itself was ripe for revolution.

THE IRAN CRISIS

The Gulistan Palace and the large foreign embassies were like giant ships in a sea of mud huts and poverty. Many Persians slept outdoors, summer and winter, with no roofs over their heads, eating grass to survive. Epidemics spread through the streets and starvation was common. Opium dens flourished in back alleyways and side streets where the depressed and apathetic Persians watched their nation slide into destruction.

In 1883, Mohammed Pahlavi's father came to this city, a young boy driving a herd of donkeys with a nail-studded stick. It didn't take long for the boy to understand the peril he was in. The city was no safer than the countryside he had left, the threat of plague or disease, or nighttime cutthroats as real as the mountain outlaws. Whatever security existed, Reza found in the presence of soldiers. He followed them through the streets, taking on small chores, running errands, listening and learning the ropes of military life. The soldiers lived a step above absolute poverty, living in dry barracks, wearing warm clothing, and eating regularly. At age fourteen, six-feet-tall Reza, the future father of Mohammed Pahlavi, enlisted in the army.

The young soldier was fearless. Thrown almost immediately into battles against the

The Shah

Persian rebels, he rode his horse into the thick of the fighting, returning from the smoke and blood the epitome of the terrible Cossack warrior, a hero to his men. By his eighteenth birthday, he had grown into a bear of a man, six-feet-six-inches-tall, his flair for leadership landing him a lieutenancy and earning him the name Reza Khan.

By nature a warrior, the young, illiterate lieutenant was nonetheless not naive to the politics around him. When Reza discovered that many of his orders came from Russia, he was scandalized. A foreign government was systematically gaining control of the army, and, through it, power over the country. Taken by a new sense of nationalism, he studied, and watched for someone to lead Persia out of her corruption and foreign entanglements.

If Reza Khan feared Russian infiltration of the army, most of his countrymen despised the British economic manipulations much more. Iranian spokesmen denounced the United Kingdom, declaring she was only using the emergency of the Great War (World War I) as an excuse to pick the nation clean. Some members of the Persian government panicked. Seeking a check on British exploitation, the Russians were welcomed with open arms.

London acted quickly. Pouring through

their dossiers, they began a search for an acceptable leader, someone strong, but not self-sufficient or capable of administration, someone controllable, and someone radically anti-Russian. They discovered Reza Khan.

The lieutenant appeared to accept London's proposal in full. With British help, he wrested control of a large division of the army and began sending home the Russian advisers.

The orders from London told Reza to stay quiet until the next move could be plotted, but the warrior had not reacted to Russian interference just to see his country fall into the hands of Great Britain. Reza Khan's massive and fearsome Persian cavalry moved immediately on Tehran, striking with such speed and daring that by the time London received the news, Khan's men had captured the palace without spilling a drop of blood.

To most observers, the new government was only a transitional one. The crude Persian peasant could not be expected to run a country. But, taking his power with deadly seriousness, Reza Khan launched extensive and long-range plans. The United Kingdom was dumbfounded. Khan began to build an army, surprising both Russia and Britain by supplying it with modern French weapons.

On December 12, 1925, the new assembly

The Shah

elected Reza Khan the "Shah of Persia." He called his ruling family the "Pahlavis," named for an ancient Persian language, and he vowed they would be a dynasty to rule Persia for generations.

It was a turbulent reign. Reza Pahlavi built his army, ruthlessly crushed all opposition, and began a campaign of "modernization" which was fiercely resisted. The whole culture was transformed. Women were forbidden to wear veils, men were ordered to cut their hair Western style.

The devoutly religious were outraged by such interference and sacrilege. The Shah's military might was tested to its limits. Talk of revolution was common. And yet, year by year, Reza Pahlavi survived.

If the cultural and religious effects of Reza Shah's "modernization" were cruel, the economic effects were spectacular. Tehran boasted wide avenues and tall buildings, though no sewers. A new Iranian railroad was built entirely without foreign aid. The University of Iran was founded. A growing constituency of peasants, soldiers, and government bureaucrats hailed the Shah as a selfless, tireless, benevolent, though strict, ruler.

In time, it was not a domestic crisis that brought down the Reza Shah's government.

THE IRAN CRISIS

From the very beginning of his rule, the capital had been festering with international intrigue. Reza had brought in German technicians to counterbalance Russian and British influence. The rise of Hitler and the threat of another world war loomed. The British insisted that the Germans go. The Shah refused.

In 1941, with German General Rommel's panzer armies threatening the Suez Canal and General Von Rundstedt's army moving into Southern Russia, the Allies suspected Iran's neutrality. They could take no chances. Russian troops entered Azerbaijan Province to the north. The British invaded from Iraq.

On the last night of the crisis, with the lights burning late at Saadabad Palace, Reza Shah huddled with his advisers, seeking to extract the best decisions in their remaining hours. They must think of the future, when, hopefully, British and Russian troops withdrew. Each step now could serve as an important precedent. Iran had come too far to slip back into anarchy and feudalism. They finally seized upon their only solution, their only hope against the future, Mohammed Reza Pahlavi, the Prince.

The young Pahlavi had lived in the tradition of Persia's earlier, less serious, princes. He had

The Shah

roamed the Mediterranean and European playgrounds, a popular figure at casinos and parties. Proud, handsome, very conscious of his royalty, he was considered by the Shah's tough, self-made associates much too soft to rule the rugged and volatile Persian kingdom. Mohammed, perfectly groomed and educated, appeared the very antithesis of the fierce Cossack warrior who had first arrived in Tehran as a starving boy in rags with a herd of donkeys.

On September 16, 1941, under the watchful eyes of British and Russian observers, Reza Shah's loyal Prime Minister Foroughi arrived at Parliament. The army was ordered to seal and guard the doors. Entering the Majlis, the prime minister slowly walked to the center, turned, and, according to the plan worked out carefully with the Allies, read his Shah's abdication speech.

Silence descended, the Russian and British ambassadors sat, staring straight ahead, expressionless. In a last rebellious gesture, the angry Majlis refused ratification.

"The doors have been locked, and are guarded," the president of the chamber advised. "You will not be allowed to leave until ratification is complete." The British and Russian diplomats expressed no uneasiness and sensed no betrayal. Let Parliament have its moment of

THE IRAN CRISIS

dignity. Let them go through their motions of a "deliberation."

Several miles away, Nedjati, one of the Shah's most trusted guards, slipped out the back door of Saadabad Palace, and, looking at the row of shiny, royal cars, selected an old beat-up Chrysler, dusty and dirty. Pulling away from the service entrance, he banged through the streets of Tehran, crisscrossing back and forth, avoiding Russian and British troops in the streets.

Prince Mohammed was waiting when the old Chrysler pulled up. "Down on the floor!" Nedjati ordered. And once more he took to the back streets, driving in circles before returning to the old Shah's Saadabad Palace, high in the hills above Tehran.

It was a poignant moment, that last farewell between father and son. The playboy prince, just barely in his twenties, stood like cold steel, prompting one of the observers to write later that even then he began to suspect there was some of the old warrior's blood in the young ruler-to-be.

"We are sending you to the Majlis," the old Shah said. "You must take the oath in time. Our guards can guarantee you only moments, but it will be enough."

Nedjati watched nervously, anxious to get

The Shah

back to the Majlis before the British or Russians became suspicious. Others in the court wept openly while Reza Shah and son faced each other, straight and tall, their emotions held firmly in check.

"I expect you to devote all your energies to stay on the throne," the old Shah said. "They'll do everything they can to push you off it. Be patient. Bend with the wind. The war will end, and when it does, you must still be king." The old Shah picked up his cane and his silver cigarette case and strode from the room, never looking back.

Mohammed Reza Pahlavi was once more rushed through the corridors of the palace, ordered back to the dirty floor of the Chrysler and whisked through the army-infested streets of Tehran.

As they approached Parliament, Nedjati skillfully zigzagged, evading any curious pursuers, until, finally, almost casually, he passed through a service gate into Parliament, sailing under the noses of the occupying armies. Dashing through an emergency entrance left unlocked by a guard, the prince was greeted by members of the old prime minister's staff. He jammed his legs into the pants of an official uniform, buttoned the jacket handed to him and followed Nedjati, racing down the hall

THE IRAN CRISIS

When Mohammed Reza entered the Majlis, the room filled with shouting and pointing and muted cheers. The onlooking British and Russian diplomats stared in shock. The prince strode to the podium and, with trembling voice and ashen face, read his oath of allegiance. His father had won, the Pahlavis had retained the throne.

Quickly spurned by the British and Russian authorities, the new Shah of Iran retreated to the far reaches of the palace, leaving the work of resistance to the aging Prime Minister Forughi. It was the Princess Ashraf, Mohammed's strong-willed twin sister, who finally provoked the reluctant Shah into action.

At Forughi's and Ashraf's instigation, the young king humbly lobbied the Allied powers for a definition of their intentions in Iran. On January 29, 1942, the Tripartite Treaty was signed, assuring Iran's political independence, promising military aid, and other economic assistance. The most important provision insisted that all foreign troops must leave Iranian territory six months after the end of hostilities between the Allies and Germany. The Shah insisted on repeated guarantees that Russia and Britain would not, some time in the future, partition Iran and take it over for themselves.

The Shah

Still suspicious and determined not to have this diplomatic move slip through his fingers, the new Shah sent his treaty directly to Stalin and Churchill for signatures. He got them. There was now a glimmer of hope that the monarchy would survive.

If the fragile Pahlavi government did have a promise that the Allies would leave Iran, there was still some question as to what they might be leaving behind. British and Russian troops played havoc with the country throughout the early 1940s. Riots continued, the British using them as a pretext to seize transportation and print new money, straddling the Iranian economy with runaway inflation. Stalin attempted to dismantle entire munitions factories and move them to Russia. In the northwestern Azerbaijan province, the Soviets established the Tudeh, the Iranian Communist Party, while, at the same time, encouraging mountainous tribes to fight for their autonomy from Tehran.

In the capital itself, the palace began to hear disquieting rumors. The British were said to be casting about for a new king, one of the corrupt Qajars. The Shah was once more prompted into action, this time appealing to the Americans.

In correspondence with President Franklin Roosevelt, Shah Mohammed Pahlavi pleaded

43

THE IRAN CRISIS

for an "American presence to save his country from the Russian menace." A long-range Iranian-American relationship was sketched out with America receiving generous concessions in return for help in developing Iran's rich natural resources. Roosevelt was seduced by the appeal for help from the young Shah. Thirty thousand American engineers and technicians arrived in Tehran and the monarchy once again survived.

If the American presence saved the Pahlavi monarchy, it did little to gain the respect of his own people. The U.S.-built airports and highways were offset by an unwanted growing American military presence.

Iran was now powerless in the presence of three mighty nations, not two. Shah Mohammed Pahlavi was criticized openly for his weakness. The Tudeh (Communist) Party was everywhere.

The Second World War finally ended, but Iran remained an armed camp. Political unrest was rampant as each sectarian interest appealed to a sympathetic foreign power to gain its ends. The Anglo-Russo-American governments themselves exploited the division. Riots shook all of the major cities. Political assassinations increased.

In public, the participating signatories of the Tripartite Treaty still spoke of evacuating Iran

The Shah

within the promised six months after the war, but privately, some argued for an indefinite presence. In late 1945, the Americans made an attempt to disengage, but Russian troops entered Tehran behind them and the new U.S. President Harry S. Truman ordered them back.

Drawing on the credibility of his Roosevelt correspondence, Shah Mohammed Pahlavi appealed to Truman. America could not just ignore a treaty it had signed, neither could it afford to leave the oil-rich kingdom to the Russians.

Truman agreed. In January, 1946, two months before the deadline, U.S. troops pulled out, the British following in March. Stalin's forces feigned a withdrawal, but remained in Azerbaijan province, poised for another move to Tehran. The American President who had dropped the atomic bomb on Japan the previous year sent the Kremlin a "blunt message." Get out of Iran within a week or America will camp permanently in the Persian Gulf.

When the problem resurfaced two years later, the Shah, impressed with the success of Truman's tough posture, dispatched a spokesman to the newly formed United Nations. Russian delegates tried to block access to the floor, but failed. Iran's case was passionately argued

THE IRAN CRISIS

and Soviet armed forces retreated back across the border.

Tehran was ecstatic. Historians could not determine a moment in recent centuries when Persia had been completely free of foreign armies. The Shah was cheered in the streets. Returning to the casinos and parlors of post-World-War-II Europe, Mohammed Reza Pahlavi was greeted as the savior of his country.

But Iran's moment of unity was short. Even without the presence of foreign troops, the nation once more moved to the brink of anarchy. Muslim mullahs continued to agitate against the "modernization" begun under Reza Shah. With the Russian withdrawal, Communist activity paradoxically picked up. The Shah was, not inaccurately, portrayed as a playboy.

On February 4, 1949, a lone assassin opened fire on Mohammed Pahlavi. It was the occasion of the fourteenth anniversary of the University of Tehran. The Shah was walking down a red carpet in a receiving line, when a man bearing press credentials ripped open his bulky, homemade camera and pulled out a pistol. For long seconds, the Shah was alone on the red carpet, twisting and ducking as the assassin's bullets whizzed by.

The bloodied Mohammed Pahlavi miracu-

The Shah

lously survived, walking into a hospital under his own strength, but the event was a turning point. The monarch's previous, carefully cultivated image of tolerance and forgiveness was abandoned. There was no pretense of due process. The Shah, still raging over his sense of helplessness before one man with a gun, demanded results. It was time to know who were the enemies of the monarchy and it was time for a showdown.

The (Communist) Tudeh bore the brunt of the king's wrath. Martial law was declared and party members were systematically rounded up. What Communist party machinery that survived went *sub rosa*, and there it stayed.

But the Shah's enthusiastic investigation turned up some surprises. The assassin's press credentials had been signed by the *Partcham Islam,* a right-wing Muslim newspaper. In the hysteria and thoroughness of the Shah's campaign, Ayatollah Kashani, director of the newspaper, was arrested. The investigation also bagged former Iranian Prime Minister Qavam, but Mohammed Pahlavi could not bring himself to believe that the enemies of the throne could be so diverse and widespread. In spite of the evidence, Qavam was given clemency and others involved in the plot were released. The Shah appeared to be backing

THE IRAN CRISIS

down from his counterattack, seeking other methods to secure the throne.

In 1949, an ambitious series of governmental reforms were announced, the monarch promising he would lead the nation to a time of great prosperity. Major economic treaties were signed with the United States, and American technicians began arriving by the thousands. That same year, a press censorship bill reached the Majlis. Remarks against the royal family would henceforth be forbidden. A month later, the Shah reactivated the Senate, making that royally appointed body equal to the elected Majlis.

But Mohammed Pahlavi's attempts to take the initiative throughout this period were hampered by a fundamental flaw. By law, Mohammed could not assume the Peacock Throne until he had a male heir. It was a technicality which did not legally interfere with his work. He was assuredly the king, but the effect of the uncertainty of the Pahlavi reign led to much intrigue and palace maneuvering. The Shah was weakened.

In 1939, at the instruction of his father, Reza Shah, Mohammed had married Fawzia, King Farouk's sister. No son and heir had been born, the marriage had failed, the prince had returned to the night life of Europe.

The Shah

In 1949, in his quest to solidify the power of the monarchy, Mohammed renounced his life as a playboy and finally addressed the problem of an heir. The Shah's sister proposed a marriage alliance with one of the rebellious tribes in the North.

On February 12, 1951, Mohammed Reza Pahlavi married Soraya Esfandiary, the elegant and strikingly beautiful daughter of a tribal leader. Soraya, though fragile in health, was swept off to the beaches and casinos of the world, while the Pahlavi family remained in the palace praying that the Shah and his bride would have a fruitful honeymoon.

In the days and months that followed, antigovernment terrorists played havoc with the country. The prime minister and the minister of education were assassinated, the latter struck down in a mosque during prayers.

Rushing home to Tehran, Mohammed Reza named Hossein Ala prime minister, but the new choice only aroused the people more. Sensing that the government was on the ropes, leftists and rightists fell into line behind a common issue. "Nationalize the oil fields, push the British out!" Huge mobs broke into the square facing Parliament. Demonstrators waved fists in the air, chanted slogans, and issued

THE IRAN CRISIS

ultimatums ordering the British-owned oil companies out of the country. The Shah himself had chafed under British exploitation. Pointing to the mobs on the streets, he warned London to strike a deal now or perhaps face a more hostile government.

Iran had once again come to the brink. The monarch had very few options. Mohammed Pahlavi resigned himself to the fact that only one man could satisfy the mobs in the streets and hope to put together a workable government. It was time to call on Mohammed Hedayat Mossadegh, the crippled, bald old man with the moon-shaped wire glasses and the Ghandian-like popularity with Persians. He had been an opponent of the Pahlavis for two generations. The palace held its breath as the Shah did the unthinkable.

Iran's new prime minister embodied many of the contradictory elements of the nation. Considered a leftist by most (he symbolically slept with red sheets), Mossadegh nonetheless had great support from rightist Muslims who admired him for his personal austerity and apparent incorruptibility.

Mossadegh had crusaded for the nationalization of oil long before it had become a popular issue. In almost Churchillian style, he had become so identified with the cause that when

The Shah

it became the cry of the nation, his power correspondingly rose. But primarily, the old man's popularity rested on the growing bitterness toward the monarchy. Mossadegh, who had been crippled in old Reza Shah's prisons, was the very symbol of the anti-Shah forces.

If the King of Iran had cause to be nervous about his popular and powerful new prime minister, there was still a basis for cooperation. It was Mohammed Pahlavi, then a young prince, who had talked old Reza Shah into releasing the crusty, trouble-making Mossadegh from prison. On yet another occasion, Mohammed had interceded and blocked the courts from sentencing the old man to another term.

Mossadegh appeared quite willing to work with the palace. Before appointing him prime minister, the Shah had extracted a critical promise. Mossadegh would not antagonize the British, who, much as their presence was mutually despised, were desperately needed. The wily old man agreed.

The Shah got an early signal of Mossadegh's style. Within twenty-four hours, the prime minister had changed his mind. The "critical promise" was broken. The British were ordered out. The oil industry would be nationalized.

If it were not for the seriousness of the situation and the insult of such contemptuous duplicity, the Shah might have been amused by the naiveté of his new prime minister. The British reacted quickly, blockading the Persian Gulf and reducing the flow of oil to a trickle. London naturally turned tough in its relationship with the Mossadegh government, tabling or postponing projects which had taken patient years to put in motion. The prime minister's quick move had not only needlessly insulted the Shah, who, unpopular as he was for the moment, had an amazing record of survivability, and had been willing to work with the irascible old politician, it had also backfired for the Iranian oil industry.

Nevertheless, Mossadegh's swift action, counterproductive and foolish as it may have seemed to the experienced Shah, aroused the nation. The new prime minister's cockiness touched something deep in the Iranian soul. Reared in the palace, Mohammed Pahlavi may have learned the complexities and nuances of dealing with a superior foreign power. Eventually, he would succeed. The Shah would secure his nation's oil fields. But, from his first day in office, Mossadegh gave the nation something she needed even more than her oil fields, her self-respect.

In 1953, after only three and a half years in

The Shah

power, the old shrunken, crippled, idealistic prime minister had obtained an iron grip in Tehran. The capital was swarming with plots against the throne. Many members of the Pahlavi family were evacuated.

On August 16, 1953, only hours before government officers were dispatched to arrest them, Mohammed Reza Pahlavi and his wife Soraya, flew a light plane across the border into neighboring Iraq. The storybook prince had fallen. The Shah of Iran was in exile.

3

The White Revolution

The Persian Empire founded by Cyrus the Great had lasted more than two hundred years. It had taken Alexander and his Greek legions to bring it down, but once fallen, Persia had never recovered. Throughout its turbulent history, the nation had suffered under a curse much like the workers in the biblical story of Babel. Uniting briefly in the face of oncoming danger, Persia would shatter into division and anarchy when within the very reach of victory. Corruption, greed and sectarian divisions devastated the most idealistic and well-intentioned government a shah could field.

And so it was that the twentieth-century government of Mohammed Mossadegh, having very briefly enjoyed an almost Ghandian-like hold over the nation, suddenly found itself

THE IRAN CRISIS

plagued with charges of corruption and scandal. There appeared to be no solutions to Iran's ancient problems. Sixty-five percent of its people were still landless serfs, bribes still oiled the otherwise glacial pace of government bureaucracy, a foreign navy still ruled the Persian Gulf. The Tudeh (Communist) Party was losing none of its appeal under Mossadegh. Western intelligence operatives watched nervously, coming to realize with each passing day that the government in Tehran was more fragile and vulnerable than the outside world had yet perceived. Iran was about to take another turn.

Mohammed Pahlavi, still shaken by his narrow escape, had no time to ponder the mysteries of Persia. Carrying only the clothes on his back, he had flown on to Rome where a poor Iranian businessman, pitying the exiled king, had loaned him an automobile and money.

Four days later, sitting with Soraya in an elegant dining room at the Hotel Excelsior, the exiled Shah was suddenly surrounded by newsmen. The government of Mohammed Mossadegh had been overthrown by a military coup. Looking out at the famous, tree-lined Via Veneto, the Shah's eyes grew moist. "I knew they loved me," he murmured. "I knew they loved me."

The White Revolution

But it was the American CIA who loved him, not the Iranian people. The United States, led by intelligence operative, Kermit Roosevelt (Franklin's grandson), had pulled the strings inside Iran's army and brought the Mossadegh government down. The Shah would have another chance.

Mohammed Pahlavi's return to the palace in Tehran marked the beginning of a new era for the nation. Having lost and regained power so quickly, he returned to duties with a new sobriety and a determination to give Iran and his own life something neither had seen much of—stability. The Shah energetically set out to reorganize the army into his own personal instrument, loyal to the throne. Long-range economic plans were discussed, plans which the Shah himself would supervise. If he could not make his people love him, he would make sure they feared and respected him.

Much has been written and debated about the years that followed. While detractors spoke of the Shah's megalomania and chafed under "police repression," none could deny the enormous energy exuded and the successful completion of so many complex projects.

Giant steel mills rose out of the desert. Tehran itself boomed to a city of two and a half million people, with streets clogged by Iranian-made vehicles. A widely diversified gross national product began to attain a ten percent annual growth, and held at that pace into the 1960s. Personal income climbed out of the basement, almost doubling to $300.00 per year.

The Shah's economic successes and powerful army notwithstanding, one very acute weakness remained for the monarchy. Mohammed Pahlavi still had no heir. Meeting with the Council of Sages in 1957, the King was admonished to sire a son quickly, or face a continuing crisis of his authority. Some favored modifying the constitution to allow a Qajar to assume the throne in the event of Pahlavi's death.

Under increasing pressure, Prime Minister Eghbal appealed to the Shah's wife, Soraya. Islamic law did not prevent a man from marrying more than one woman, and, indeed, specifically provided for a second wife in order to bear an heir. Would Her Highness object if the King took a second wife? Soraya was infuriated!

At a night club, days later, the royal marriage crisis surfaced. Knowing of her husband's much publicized preference for long-legged blondes, and watching the former playboy dance throughout the evening with just such a European woman, Soraya fled into the night.

The White Revolution

At the palace, the beautiful, temperamental daughter of a tribal chieftain summoned attendants and spent the evening before the giant fireplace in her palace apartment, tossing the Shah's love letters and pictures into the flames.

Learning days later that his wife had fled to the glamorous Swiss ski resort of St. Moritz, the Shah dispatched army generals to negotiate a way for his wife's return. But there would be no reconciliation. Soraya's answer was final.

The King's second divorce took place amidst official palace mourning. Throughout Iran the Royal Empress's picture was ordered down and, in its place, was displayed a "document of poetry and regret," written by the Shah himself.

Mohammed Pahlavi, angry with the forces which lost him his marriage, and sincerely mourning the loss of Soraya, once more tabled his own personal domestic problems and poured himself into the grand projects which would lift his nation out of the past.

But as a king, and as one of the world's richest, single human beings, the Shah was too much of a catch to remain single. At a royal party in Paris, he was introduced to a delegation of Iranian students. The youths were awed, except for one Farah Diba, who shocked the party by publicly challenging the King's decision to reduce scholarship grants for Iranians studying abroad. Mohammed Pahlavi only smiled back at the spirited coed while government officials rushed him on by.

On December 21, 1959, the Shah of Iran married the beautiful Farah Diba in the Hall of Mirrors at the Marble Palace in Tehran. At last the King found a fruitful womb. Amidst wide celebration, Crown Prince Reza Cyrus was born the following year. Once again, the monarchy had been saved.

Returning to his long-range schedule for the westernization of Iran, in 1963, the Shah announced his "White Revolution." Land would be redistributed from the "rich to the poor," and workers would own shares in the companies that employed them.

In the Western media, the plan was richly applauded. The government began by parceling out all of the Shah's own lands, then by buying large tracts of territory from feudal landlords and dividing them among peasants.

But in Iran, there was turmoil. Few of the peasants became landowners. The others, an enormous mass of farm workers and herdsmen who had been granted food sources and credit under the ancient system, now struggled to

The White Revolution

determine their new status. Thousands sold their new property to finance a once-in-a-lifetime pilgrimage to one of Iran's two holy cities, Qum or Mashed. Impoverished materially, but considering themselves spiritually nurtured, the destitute peasants thronged to the cities, to become part of a wretched mass trying to eke out an existence by menial labor in industry.

Most significantly, the Muslim mullahs once again became aroused. Most had violently condemned the "modernization" of Iran begun by Reza Shah. Especially galling had been the women's rights emphasis under Mohammed Pahlavi. But the land redistribution program posed a jugular threat to the Shiite Muslim clergy. Large properties administered by the mullahs were broken up. Donations, which had previously come from feudal landlords, trailed off.

In June of 1963, the White Revolution turned red. Aroused by the fiery sermons of an old Muslim preacher who had recently attained the holy title of Ayatollah, riots broke out in major cities. The bazaar in Tehran was set ablaze.

The Shah of Iran reacted swiftly. Army commandos and SAVAK secret police agents descended on the sixty-three-year-old preacher's home in the holy city of Qum. The Ayatollah Ruhollah Khomeini was thrown into prison, an act which only strengthened his growing popularity. Within weeks, the old man was put on a plane and flown to Turkey, where authorities immediately deported him to Iraq.

The Ayatollah Khomeini's sermons, smuggled back into Iran, were a small impediment to the great rush toward modernization. From 1965 through 1970, American businessmen poured one hundred and fifty million investment dollars into the country. In 1969, a thirty-three-million-dollar caustic soda plant opened in Abadan, one-fourth of it owned by the American B.F. Goodrich Company. In 1970, the Iranian government became equal partners with Allied Chemical in a two-hundred-forty-million-dollar project. Reynolds Metals Company built a forty-five million-dollar aluminum plant in Arak, western Iran. In Tehran, the Caterpillar Tractor Company opened a ten-million-dollar service headquarters, one of the largest in the world, and necessary to maintain the giant yellow land movers and graders that were bulldozing Iran into a modern nation.

Spectacular as the foreign investments were, Iran's economy began to heat up. In 1969, pri-

The White Revolution

ces rose 3.6 percent, twice the rate of previous years, a portent of the future. A rise in the price of oil appeared to be one way to offset the decline in Iranian purchasing power, but the American-European Consortium that accounted for ninety percent of Iran's sales warned that there was a limit to the income that could be squeezed out of oil. The nine American-European oil companies, negotiating with the Shah, increased Iran's 1970 share of the oil receipts to $1.150 billion.

Increasingly, worldwide, Iran was gaining the reputation as a stable force in the volatile Middle East. In 1968, the British navy steamed out of the Persian Gulf, prompting the Shah to announce plans for a militarily strong Iran.

Though detractors attributed it to Mohammed Pahlavi's megalomania or referred to the arms as personal toys of the Shah, Iran's huge military buildup had historic justification. Iran had been subjected to humiliation and servitude by countless foreign armies literally since its fall to Greece, hundreds of years before; now the Shah saw a chance for her to break free.

Iran promised to be the fifth-ranking world power by 1985. And, while this grandiose announcement brought smiles to the faces of Western generals, there was soon respect for the growing Persian arsenal. In eight years, the Shah spent almost four billion dollars on military purchases from the United States alone. A 1973 shopping list included Phantom fighter bombers, doubling his air force to three hundred fifty combat planes. That same year, the Shah bought seven hundred British-made Centurion tanks, a purchase that exceeded that of both the French and British.

In Iran, there was resentment and fear. People resented the military ascendancy that gave soldiers free automobiles and high wages, and they feared the growing military might which could forever seal their fate with the Shah.

It was difficult for outsiders to comprehend the passionate opposition to Mohammed Reza Pahlavi in his own land. Over the years, textbooks had sung his praises, his picture was posted on every street, censored newspapers faithfully reported his many achievements. Still, in moments of greatest triumph, there was always a festering threat to the throne.

Part of the problem lay with the Tudeh, whose thirst would only be sated by complete control. But, contrary to the Shah's tendency to attribute all his woes to Communist agitation, there were other enemies of the monarchy, even besides the old mullahs, whose roar was

The White Revolution

beginning to sound like that of a toothless lion to the government.

Among the many newly educated and wealthy Iranians was much frustration with bureaucratic corruption, the ruthless repression by the SAVAK, and manipulated elections. Special resentment was held for the Shah's family, whose extensive business empire provided numerous ways to extract bribes and favors.

Ironically, the Shah's own personal extravagance was outrageous to many of the very families who were themselves advancing due to his economic magic tricks. His Majesty owned five palaces and a Swiss villa formerly belonging to actress Audrey Hepburn. When the Shah traveled, it sometimes required three jets, one Boeing 707 for luggage alone. Persons were required to stand when he entered a room, subjects kissed his hand, and peasants, who were supposed to show respect for the father of the "White Revolution," were expected to kiss his feet. Nixon's Treasury Secretary William Simon called the Shah of Iran a "nut."

In October, 1971, Mohammed Pahlavi hosted a spectacular twenty-five hundredth anniversary celebration of the Persian empire. Nine kings and sixteen presidents flew to the desert pageant in Persepolis. It was a hundred-million-dollar extravaganza.

From exile in Iraq, the old Ayatollah Khomeini fiercely denounced the Shah and his corruption, reminding whoever would listen that, while the greatest chefs in the world were mixing recipes under extravagant, air-conditioned royal tents placed in the middle of the desert, and the King's guard was outfitted in thousand-dollar Lanvin-designed uniforms, the peasants of the Persepolis region were in the midst of a famine. The message got no press, but it was a poignant point to the few of the mullah's disciples who heard it.

Other extravagances proved even more difficult to rationalize. The poor Iranian businessman who had kindly loaned his car and money to the Shah during the 1953 exile had been rewarded with his nation's Pepsi-Cola franchise and was now building a replica of the Petit Trianon at Versailles. The palace was reportedly costing more than fifteen million dollars.

Amid resentment and frustration, Iran's economic miracle had nevertheless continued. Annual per capita income increased to $480.00 per year. A massive hundred-thousand-member "literacy corps" was sent into the countryside. By 1973, eighty-five percent of the

The White Revolution

nation's villages had participated in land redistribution. The gross national product had doubled in one decade. In one twelve-month period, more than two million new jobs were created.

But "the miracle" of the sixties and early seventies would soon be dwarfed by the economic news of 1974. The previous year, Shah Mohammed Reza Pahlavi had agreed to sell most of Iran's future oil to European and American companies in return for their pledge to turn over their operations to the government. When the oil-producing economic cartel emerged, the Shah, representing the second largest oil-producing nation in the world, pushed for the very highest prices. Iran reaped a fortune. Oil income which amounted to five billion dollars in 1973 jumped almost five hundred percent to twenty-three billion dollars in 1974, with no end in sight. The gross national product increased by an incredible fifty percent in one year. In a 1974 interview, the King of Iran could boast that his nation's farmers owned their own land, workers could buy shares in their own factories, studies were free and the government subsidized food.

If the Shah had difficulty in developing respect from his own people, the Western world was beginning to appreciate what was

THE IRAN CRISIS

happening to the awakened Iran and there was not universal agreement that it was a good thing. Leftist Iranians may have scorned government statistics showing progress, but Western motorists who had to wait in line to buy the now expensive gasoline needed no more evidence to believe in Iran's economic miracle. Clearly, somebody was making a lot of money. When Iran began to use its profits to reinvest in the West, there was manifest resentment. The Shah's government bought twenty-five percent of Germany's powerful Krupp Steel Corporation for one hundred million dollars. British and American banks and real estate were gobbled up, driving prices even higher for Westerners already grumbling about inflation.

Ironically, the Western world had been enthusiastic evangelists of the free enterprise system, decrying charges of exploitation and insisting that hard work and efficiency could offset any historic or natural handicaps. The Iran of Mohammed Reza Pahlavi had begun to play that game and many didn't like it.

If there was some resentment among the Western populace, there was downright enthusiasm among the diplomats. There was enormous geo-political value in a stable Iran, even if there was an economic price for the West to

The White Revolution

pay. The Shah's army had proven its mettle. Responding to a call from Oman, on the other side of the Persian Gulf, Iran's modern helicopter air cavalry had put down leftist guerrillas. The strategic Strait of Hormuz, through which most of the world's oil passed, seemed relatively safe if Iran remained strong. Henry Kissinger's "twin pillar policy" of a strong Saudi Arabia and Iran was held as the best hope to defuse a highly dangerous Middle East. The Pentagon, reminding people who would listen that the Shah's order of eighty F-14's saved the Grumann Aircraft Company from bankruptcy, declared American-Iranian cooperation critical to the defense of the United States. If all of Iran's aircraft orders were filled in 1980, she would have an air force larger than any of the NATO nations, except for the United States.

And, so, Mohammed Pahlavi had shed his image as a playboy. His monarchy was thought to be unassailable, a fact to be dealt with. In the style of American presidents, Kennedy and Johnson, the Shah had given an umbrella tag to his many economic and military plans, calling them "The Great Civilization." Superpowers, East and West, conceded with fascination that events, natural resources, and not a

THE IRAN CRISIS

little bit of skillful administration by the Shah and his latest prime minister, Mr. Hoveida, might allow the Persian Gulf state to attain its pompous claim.

4

The Rise of Khomeini

Iran's so-called "stability" was an illusion. The red-hot, 1974 economy soon began to experience the kind of inflation normally associated with South American states. Tehran, which had doubled to a city of five million, was crowded with workers who grudgingly gave away their wages on $1,500-a-month rent.

The land redistribution program, noble as it had sounded on paper, was failing. The government had tried to help by organizing the small peasant farms into giant corporations, but the government bureaucracy brought in to run things fell prey to the same old corruption. The White Revolution left Iran importing eighty percent of her food needs, while the farms produced luxurious artichokes and asparagus for export to Europe. Fear and resentment of the Shah's SAVAK grew. Riots broke out in major cities and the Shah's jails began to fill up with political prisoners.

Western advisers recommended that His Majesty "liberalize" his regime, allow more dissent, and move more quickly toward democracy. In 1976, ever seeking to mollify his critics, the tireless Shah loosened censorship, cut back SAVAK operations, and encouraged open political debate.

Indeed, the government's liberalization program momentarily neutralized critics, but within months, leftist student organizations, operating openly, began to see spectacular growth. Calling themselves "Islamic-Marxists," the movement mixed the most popular elements of the old and the new. Many of the organizers traced roots back to the government of leftist Mohammed Mossadegh, but at least one organization, the People's Mojahedeen Party, had direct links with Moscow, proving that the Shah of Iran's paranoia of Communist conspiracies was not without some justification.

It was still the potential Islamic revolution which posed the greatest threat to the monarchy. Throughout 1977, Muslim fanatics began importing tape cassettes from the old preacher exiled in Iraq. More angry and bitter in his denouncements of the Shah than ever, the seventy-

The Rise of Khomeini

seven-year-old Ayatollah Khomeini urged the people not to compromise. "The Shah must go!"

In October, 1977, the Ayatollah's forty-nine-year-old son, Seyyed Mustafa Khomeini, died. The government in Tehran said it was a heart attack, but the exiled preacher accused the Shah of murder. The story was debated in pamphlets and newspaper editorials. By the beginning of 1978, there were continuous anti-government demonstrations in Qum.

While the angry old teacher in exile preached the most radical anti-Shah messages, most Shiite Muslims looked to the Ayatollah Sharietmadari as the true leader of the movement. At eighty-one years of age, Sharietmadari was renown throughout the Islamic world as one of their foremost scholars. He was a kindly, bespectacled old man who, at first, was labeled by "palace experts" as too "tender" to be a substantial threat.

When Sharietmadari called for a demonstration in his holy city of Qum, thousands appeared. Police fired on the crowd, killing nine. There was a forty-day truce as supporters of the old mullah obeyed Islamic traditions of mourning, and then took to the streets. Confrontations with police escalated. More demonstrators died. On May 10, 1978, government paratroopers, led by a major general, broke

THE IRAN CRISIS

into Sharietmadari's Qum headquarters. The holy man and his disciples were having prayers when the paratroopers began firing their weapons. It was only a warning, but, before the government troops left, one theology student lay on the Ayatollah's rug, bleeding to death. Another died in the hospital the next day.

The nation's Muslims awakened in fury. The Shah was touching "the holy ones." Pictures of the radical Ayatollah Khomeini began to appear in the streets. While the scholarly and patient Sharietmadari took a step closer to the angry, exiled Khomeini, there was still no call for a *jihad*, a holy war, from Qum.

At his Spartan headquarters, the Ayatollah Sharietmadari sat lotus style, greeting delegations of political and student leaders. With blood stains on the rugs and a bullet-shredded curtain dramatically hanging behind him, the Muslim Shiite leader counseled moderation. He reiterated his call to return to the 1906 Constitution, to reduce the King to a figurehead, and place a five-man council of mullahs with veto power as Islamic advisers to Parliament.

The people found it very difficult to wait. On June 5, Muslim leaders called for a series of national strikes that closed several cities, including much of Tehran. Mobs in the streets battled

The Rise of Khomeini

police, resulting in forty deaths.

Having patiently survived his enemies for years, the Shah calmly began to neutralize the Islamic movement. Pornographic motion pictures were banned. The despised royal family was reined in, their businesses ordered to adhere to a strict code of ethics. Prime ministers were shuffled around like musical chairs. And still, there were sizable anti-government tremors, warning that any efforts might be too late.

On August 1, 1978, students and workers demonstrated at the home of the Ayatollah Khademi in Isfahan. Under army threats, Khademi bravely tried to restrain the crowd, urging Sharietmadari's moderation, but it was to no avail. Having grown into the thousands, the mob left the cautious Khademi, rampaging through the streets. As in the demonstrations in Qum and Tehran, pictures of the radical Khomeini began to appear.

By August 11, literally hundreds of thousands of Iranians rioted in the streets of Isfahan. Police and army units lost two hundred vehicles in their battle with the mobs. Martial law was declared.

The following week, the Rex Cinema in Abadan burned to the ground, taking four hundred people with it. The massacre, definitely the work of arsonists, was blamed on

"Islamic fanatics" and condemned around the world. In Iran, word spread that the film was subtly anti-Pahlavi, that, reminiscent of the Reichstag fire, the government itself had set the blaze as either a warning or a pretext to begin an anti-Islamic crusade. Massive rioting broke out spontaneously across Iran. On September 8 alone, unofficial reports listed fifteen hundred deaths. The eighty-one-year-old Ayatollah Sharietmadari began to openly speak revolution while seeking to keep the mobs nonviolent and under control.

Once more, the Shah moved to appease the Islamic movement. Jaafar Sharif-Emami, a devout Muslim, was named prime minister. The Islamic calendar was restored, gambling was shut down, the governmental Department for Women's Affairs was eliminated, press censorship was totally lifted, and several prominent religious leaders, imprisoned during the riots, were set free.

The patient, kindly Ayatollah Kazem Sharietmadari was not totally mollified, but he approved of the progress, apologetically assuring Western reporters that there would be no armed insurrection. When the Shah publicly invited the other Ayatollah back from his exile in Iraq, Khomeini only issued a new message to his followers, scornfully rejecting the Shah's invitation

The Rise of Khomeini

and calling for a jihad—holy war—against the Pahlavi regime.

On September 21, the Shah's dreaded SAVAK agents began rounding up dissidents. More than a thousand were bagged, including the Ayatollah Yahya Noori. The street activity fell for a few days, and then exploded in even greater fury.

Iran was on the brink. Wherever the guilt lay and whatever the injustice, the facts were that the Shah of Iran had lost his people. When Muslim leaders called for new strikes, the country was brought to a virtual standstill. In October of 1978, with airlines grounded, the nation's mail collecting dust, and his rich oil fields idled by the strike, the King of Iran struck back at his aging tormentor. Pressure was put on the Iraqis to deport the Ayatollah Khomeini. The old mullah was once more a prophet without a "place to lay his head."

First denied entrance into Kuwait, Khomeini slipped into France. Settling in a Parisian suburb, the seventy-eight-year-old voice of the radical opposition started up again. Western newsmen, fascinated and amused by the exotic, ascetic life style of the old mullah, flocked to his tiny apartment in Neauphle-le-Chateau. They got up with Khomeini at 2:00 A.M., sat patiently as he prayed under a nearby apple tree, and carefully logged the numerous political and religious delegations that paid their respects. Some Westerners developed affection for the gutsy "old man." Many Iranians living in Europe expressed great pity for the Ayatollah, who, in Paris, had no mosque. "He is fearless," one said, "and sometimes I agree with him, but they will never let him come home."

On November 1, the government crisis mounting each day, the strikes threatening to undo the economic achievements of a decade, Mohammed Reza Pahlavi began conversations with his former enemies. A coalition government, involving all elements of Persian society and politics, was still believed to be a possible solution. The Shah's concessions were generous. The moderate Ayatollah Sharietmadari was secretly briefed, the throne still counting on his tenuous leadership of the Islamic movement. But Sharietmadari's power was slipping.

Karim Sanjabi, leader of the *National Front* and heir to the Mossadegh following, was the Shah's most successful catch. Sanjabi, only recently released from one of the Shah's detention cells, decided to cooperate if "conditions were met." The state of the nation was serious. Something had to be done quickly if anything at all could be salvaged. Only one obstacle, the exiled Ayatollah, remained to a coalition gov-

The Rise of Khomeini

ernment that would defuse the mobs in the street. On November 3, Sanjabi made his pilgrimage to France. But the stubborn Ayatollah Khomeini would not budge. First, the idolatrous Shah must go.

Mohammed Pahlavi's latest plan to launch a government was quickly struck down by events. Khomeini's orders, telephoned to Tehran, called for no letup in the strikes and demonstrations. On November 4, students at the university toppled a statue of the Shah. Government troops herded the mob back into the campus, but, by the following morning, the demonstrations had reassembled. This time there was gunfire. Several students lay dying on the streets. The mob rose in fury. Banks and theaters were burned. The British embassy was destroyed, sending London's diplomats scurrying across town. The Shah's prime minister resigned and the military took over.

In a nationwide television address Monday, November 6, a contrite Mohammed Pahlavi pleaded for order. "What is most critical," he said, "the lifeline of our country, the flow of oil, has been interrupted." Referring to "the sacrifices you have made," the Shah pledged that the new military regime must restore order and "do away" with corruption. "Let us think of Iran on the road against imperialism, cruelty,

and corruption, where I shall accompany you."
Mohammed Pahlavi had apparently joined the revolution.

The military regime moved with dispatch. Former Prime Minister Hoveida, the man who had ruled for an unprecedented thirteen years and who saw much of the nation's economic growth, was arrested. When Karim Sanjabi returned from his rendezvous with Khomeini, he, too, was arrested. The old mullah in Paris was unimpressed. Khomeini called for massive demonstrations on forthcoming Muslim holy days.

In December, 1978, the holy month of Muhurram on the Islamic calendar, Khomeini's mobs and the new military government had their showdown. On December 11, hundreds of thousands of students, and workers, and women wrapped in their full-length, black *chadors* marched along Shahreza Avenue in downtown Tehran. The parade reached Shahyad Square, where, under the massive, ten-million-dollar arch built to the glory of Mohammed Pahlavi, the crowd held high pictures of seventy-eight-year-old Ayatollah Khomeini and shouted, "Death to the Shah!"

The King of Iran cloistered himself in his palace at the foot of the glorious Elburz mountains. Aides admitted that the Shah was lonely

The Rise of Khomeini

and in a state of deep "shock." "He needs lots of stroking," a palace source said. President Carter's foreign adviser, Zbigniew Brzezinski, telephoned American assurances, no matter which direction the Shah turned. Meanwhile, the crown's massive 280,000-man army stood on alert. Two hundred tanks positioned themselves at strategic points throughout the city, one division forming an awesome row of artillery power just in front of the walls to the Shah's palace.

But the outcome in Iran was still uncertain. When three pro-Khomeini soldiers entered an army mess hall only blocks from the palace and opened fire, killing six, there was a backlash of sympathy for the Shah's army. A persistent rumor among the Islamic community had it that the Ayatollah Qumi had been visited by the ancient saint Imam Reza in a dream. The Muslim holy man of Mashed was worried that Ayatollah Khomeini was pitting Muslim brother against brother.

State Department officials in Washington, D.C., were overwhelmed with the ramifications of a possible Islamic government in Iran. A Khomeini regime would be radically anti-American. The exiled Ayatollah had already warned that a "pure" Islamic republic must immediately cut off oil to the infidel Americans

THE IRAN CRISIS

and Zionist Israelis. Jerusalem looked to Iran for seventy percent of her crude oil, the United States eight percent.

Washington's greatest fear was the Soviet response to a Pahlavi fall from power. The Russians had already sent one billion dollars worth of military equipment into Ethiopia. They had growing facilities in South Yemen. The government ruling from Kabul, Afghanistan, was pro-Moscow. One look at the map sent shivers down any casual Western student of geo-politics. It could be no coincidence; from both sides, the Russian bear was closing in on the strategic Hormuz Straits. Would a shaky leftist Islamic government in Tehran unwittingly fulfill Nikita Khruschev's prophecy of decades past? "We will never have to take Iran," the Russian premier had said, "she will rot away and fall into our laps."

George Ball, former Undersecretary of State for John Kennedy, was commissioned by the White House to prepare a paper on the future of the Persian Gulf. The assignment triggered a legion of rumors among the Georgetown set. Newsmen speculated that the paper included a contingency plan for a post-Pahlavi Iran. The White House firmly denied it.

President Carter, on the final week of the year, announced that he fully expected "the

The Rise of Khomeini

Shah to maintain power" and that the Iranian crisis would be resolved. The President's comment caused great concern in Tehran where the Shah's aides warned that "Jimmy Carter must not be fully briefed on the situation here." Jerusalem was angry. A business friend of Menachem Begin's said that Carter's successful, even spectacular, performance at Camp David notwithstanding, the American President appeared to be "very naive" in his understanding of the current situation in the Middle East.

Lower echelon State Department officials leaked word to American newsmen that their boss, Cyrus Vance, was totally involved in the SALT Treaty. "Very little time is spent on Iran." At the White House, Carter adviser Brzezinski was said to be running the show.

Meanwhile, in his small cottage at Neauphle-le-Chateau, the Ayatollah Khomeini issued his year-end message, ominously warning the Shah's soldiers to "flee your barracks." Embarrassed French authorities hinted that when the old man's tourist visa expired January 6, it would not be renewed.

The situation in Iran was chaotic. Battles between street mobs and soldiers flared into the open and subsided, but each time, they reached new peaks. The strikes were beginning to affect even the peasants.

THE IRAN CRISIS

Tehran's rich citizens began transferring billions of dollars out of the country. The first week of January, eight thousand foreigners left Iran, five thousand of them Americans. The airport was crammed with people sleeping on benches, wheeling and dealing with airline personel, trying to buy a ticket out of the city.

In January, 1979, the Shah formed a new government. It would be his last. Sixty-three-year-old Shahpour Bakhtiar, an outspoken opponent of the Pahlavis, was called to the palace. The 1906 Constitution that the Ayatollah Sharietmadari had called for would be put into effect. The nation's budget would be turned over to the government's cabinet. A committee of Shiite mullahs would have veto power over legislation, but the 280,000-man army would still be the Shah's.

The Bakhtiar government began on shaky ground. Only days before, President Carter had sent a carefully worded statement of support for the Shah. The statement was so weak that some capitals were interpreting it as a substantial change in U.S. policy. Pahlavi aides were stunned. The rug had been pulled out from underneath their feet.

Bakhtiar exhibited great skill in going through the motions of the chief executive. Oil would be cut off to both Israel and South Africa, the

The Rise of Khomeini

prime minister promised. Iran would support the rights of Palestinians. The SAVAK would be curtailed.

The world of Mohammed Reza Pahlavi was crumbling. The Shah's mother was reportedly on a Boeing 747 bound for Los Angeles. The King himself, in a gesture designed to endear him to his people and neutralize persistent claims on his own personal aggrandizement at the nation's expense, gave away sixty million dollars to the Pahlavi Foundation. German magazines estimated his remaining fortune at twenty-two billion dollars, but Pahlavi family members openly laughed at the figure. "He is not a rich man," a palace aide said with a straight face. Bakhtiar announced that the King may soon be leaving the country. U.S. Secretary of State Vance concurred, referring to the Shah's possible trip as a much needed "vacation." Khomeini warned that any nation keeping the Shah would receive no oil from an Islamic Iran. Switzerland, the Shah's annual vacation spot, quickly advised Tehran that their country could not guarantee the King's safety.

In the last weeks of January, the United States finally began to stir. The *U.S. Constellation* and two destroyers were positioned to move into the Persian Gulf, ostensibly to protect

THE IRAN CRISIS

American citizens still in Iran. When a U.S. oil executive was murdered, thousands more Americans fled.

The most confusing signal from Washington was the sudden appearance of Air Force General Robert Huyser in the Iranian capital. The Shah, still publicly backed by the American government, was not informed of the visit. Washington accounted for Huyser's mission as one of "propping" up the military to support Bakhtiar. The U.S. Air Force general was allegedly seeking to head off a military coup from either the right or the left. But at least two Iranian soldiers present at some of Huyser's talks got the very opposite impression. Some in Tehran saw the United States as warning the Iranian military not to intervene, either by defending the Shah's new government or by taking matters into its own hands. Palace rumors had the United States jumping ship on Pahlavi, hoping to ingratiate itself with an Islamic government which seemed increasingly probable. With Huyser still in Iran, the Shah and his Farah fled the country.

But the power to give or take the Peacock Throne was no longer America's, if, indeed, it ever had been. The people now ruled the streets. In Tabriz, the northern provincial capital of

The Rise of Khomeini

Azerbaijan, Bakhtiar's government had totally withdrawn. The Ayatollah Sharietmadari's call for nonviolence and cooperation only succeeded in driving the people deeper into the radical Muslim camp. The battle was over. The anointing had left Qum, the power was no longer in Tehran. From his humble cottage in suburban Paris, the old exiled mullah with the quickly expiring tourist visa was calling the shots.

In January, the face of the seventy-nine-year-old Ayatollah Ruhollah Khomeini began to appear in magazines and on television in the Western world. He was like some apparition from the past. At Neauphle-le-Chateau, only a short distance from the home of sex symbol Brigitte Bardot, newsmen huddled around the absurd figure as he lectured them about the necessity of women to return to the chador and to be properly "veiled." Sitting cross-legged, wrapped in his robes and turban, like mullahs centuries before him, Khomeini answered Western newsmen's questions about the future of his country with short lessons on Islamic law and faith.

In Iran, the streets were still in the hands of the mobs. Khomeini's picture was appearing everywhere. When the sun fell, excited whispers floated from housetop to housetop. "He is

THE IRAN CRISIS

coming! He is coming!"

The Bakhtiar government fired a few parting salvos. On January 25, the Tehran airport was closed to prevent the Ayatollah's return. The reaction was massive. Hundreds of thousands of Iranians rushed into the streets. After three days of demonstrations, the mob attacked the police headquarters. Thirty-seven were killed and hundreds wounded.

In the few remaining hours of January, 1979, the Shah's last government, finally convinced of its inability to govern, began to shred its secrets and pack its bags. Bakhtiar ordered the airport opened. The palaces and huge government buildings of the Pahlavi dynasty became empty and quiet. A small sprinkling of secretaries and clerks continued business as usual, their noises echoing loudly in the huge, almost empty, government chambers. There was no sense of urgency, no sign of panic, like the calm before a storm. In the distance one could hear the dull thunder of the masses shouting, "God is Great!" The righteous and angry Ayatollah Khomeini was on his way to Tehran. The idolater would be judged. The thief would lose his hand, the adulteress her head, and evil would be purged from the land. The storm was almost upon them.

5

Showdown with Carter

There is a messianic mystery among Shiite Muslims. Beginning with the Prophet Mohammed himself, authority was passed down to succeeding Imams. But the twelfth prophet-leader disappeared in 940 A.D. Shiites expect his return to lead the faithful to a period of Islamic justice and purity.

"Be sure, the Imam is going to come someday," the Ayatollah Sharietmadari told a faithful audience that January. Then, referring to the rumors that Khomeini himself is in fact the twelfth Imam, Sharietmadari added, "but he will not arrive in a Boeing 747."

Nevertheless, the welcome home for the exiled Ayatollah Ruhollah Khomeini could not have been any more awesome if he had, indeed, been the long awaited "hidden" successor to Mohammed. An ocean of cheering, exultant masses filled Tehran, trapping the old holy man's motorcade in the downtown streets and forcing a dramatic helicopter rescue. As he was carried off into the sky above them, the amazed crowd watched with awe and shouted loudly, "Alla Akhbar! Alla Akhbar!" as if it were Khomeini's righteousness which gave miraculous flight and not the American machine purchased by the now deposed Shah.

True to his promises and acting very much in the role of Mohammed's successor, which his followers were already claiming, the Ayatollah immediately called for a return to the ancient Islamic code. Within the first ten days, forty persons passed through the Revolutionary Committees and were executed before firing squads. Some were declared guilty of crimes under the Shah's regime; others had been accused of rape or homosexuality. Persons caught with alcoholic beverages were publicly flogged, women were ordered to "be veiled" and wear the chador, males and females were separated in schools.

When Mehdi Bazargan, the Ayatollah's hand-picked prime minister, openly criticized the ruthless revolutionary courts, Khomeini shot back, in a speech from Qum, "You are weak, sir!"

Showdown with Carter

But, as with other popular leaders of Iran, the euphoria was interrupted with clouds. In early March, thousands of women demonstrated for their right to wear Western dresses or blue jeans. Astonished Western newsmen began to hear street slogans from the women, "Down with Khomeini!" Showing a rare streak of flexibility, the Ayatollah backed off. Women could wear what they wished but self-appointed Revolutionary thugs made life miserable for many women who "defiled" themselves with Western clothes.

Meanwhile, in Kurdistan, sectarian dreams of autonomy reemerged and open warfare broke out. Several hundred died in clashes with the army and the Revolutionary militia. The Sunni Muslim province of Baluchistan quarreled with the exclusivity of Khomeini's Shiite interpretation of the faith and the thirteen million Turks of Azerbaijan began to agitate with Qum just as they had with Pahlavi.

Most troubling of all, the Iranian economy was in a shambles. The screws had been tightened to bring down—virtually bankrupt—the government of the Shah. Now Khomeini had inherited the destruction he himself had sown. It would take time to come back, and much of what had been lost could never be recovered. Naive mobs of Iranians, led to believe their poverty came at the hands of Western imperialism, expected to suddenly partake of the legendary oil income of the Shah and his chosen elite. Each week that passed brought greater disillusionment. Khomeini did little to reassure them with comments about the deceit of Western materialism. Many people were quite willing to be "deceived."

It was the mystique of Khomeini, the sheer energy of his personality, that allowed him to retain power at all. It was with national and religious pride the people had applauded his outspoken contemptuousness of "foreigners and infidels." There was a vicarious thrill in hearing Khomeini bait the world's great powers. What could they do, deny him their jet fighters, or refrigerators, or computers? They had nothing to tempt him with. Could they kill him? He could receive no greater honor than martyrdom.

And so it was, that when Khomeini began to step up his call for the return of the Shah and his money, the masses once again responded. It was not the new materialist middle class, or the Kurds, or the women who answered his call; the same real problems simmered. But, like Nixon's silent majority of the early seventies, Khomeini's legions were still out there and, when he spoke, they responded.

Showdown with Carter

In retrospect, it is easy for observers in the Western democracies to attribute to Khomeini the political nature of their own leaders. The Ayatollah's demand for the Shah was said to be a "trick," a political ploy to distract the people from the many failures of his government. The Shah himself discounted this theory, commenting in disgust that Khomeini just wasn't that "smart."

Actually, the Ayatollah was proceeding according to plans which he had been announcing for years. Like Hitler's *Mein Kampf,* his record was there for anyone to read.

Mohammed Reza Pahlavi had settled in Cuernavaca, Mexico, and, by the time Khomeini's new "return the Shah" crusade had begun in October, 1979, he was in no position to go anywhere. For six years a victim of lymphoma, he was being told by doctors that he should go immediately to the United States for tests. The Shah, shivering with chills and fever, waited as doctors and American diplomats debated the next move.

Even if one allowed for the facts that the Shah was terminally ill and only America could provide the sophisticated treatment needed, it was a calculated risk to let him in. The State Department had specific warnings

THE IRAN CRISIS

from its personnel at the American embassy. Give the Shah a visa and you place the whole embassy in jeopardy.

On the other hand, denying him admittance was equally unacceptable. In the first place, such a denial would have been viewed by some as inhumane. The Shah was dying. America could not refuse treatment. More importantly, Washington could not be seen as betraying a long-standing friend and ally. Carter's record was already on shaky ground in many world capitals in this regard. Turning abruptly on the Shah would send a danger signal to Third World leaders that would be unmistakable.

The final argument in favor of admitting the Shah came, ironically, from the government of Iran itself. Three separate times, Prime Minister Mehdi Bazargan assured the State Department he would protect the U.S. embassy from attack. The last of these assurances came after the Shah had been admitted and the mobs in Tehran had once again taken to the streets in violent protest.

There was precedent for Carter and his advisers to believe these assurances. Had not the embassy been seized by anti-American protesters the previous February? And had not Bazargan's government moved quickly to remove them and turn control of the embassy

Showdown with Carter

back to the United States?

But the problem lay with the question of who was ruling in Tehran. The new prime minister was on fragile ground. The real power in Iran was elusive. One day it issued from fanatical Muslim mobs and the next day the Ayatollah Ruhollah Khomeini or his fifteen-man Revolutionary Council. The American State Department accepted assurances from Bazargan, but the prime minister's power was almost bankrupt.

When the U.S. embassy was assaulted and occupied on November 4, true to his promise, Bazargan moved to intervene. On November 6, when it became apparent that Khomeini's support was with the militants, Bazargan resigned in frustration. The Imam was pleased. The prime minister had been an inconvenience he could do without. Khomeini immediately turned over the reins of government to the shadowy and secretive Revolutionary Council.

So, the stage was set for what was to become a war of nerves between an American president who, rightly or wrongly, was dangerously perceived by much of the world as weak-willed and timid, and an aging, single-purposed, Islamic fanatic, who was both the political and religious leader of his people.

When Carter began his moves to begin dialogue with Iran, Khomeini asserted two preconditions. First, the United States would have to return the Shah to Iran to face "revolutionary justice," and second, the United States would have to stop "espionage against the revolution." This last theme became particularly ominous for the hostages. The militants accused them of being spies and threatened them with trials for their "espionage."

Soon after Khomeini returned from his "rest" on November 13, Washington and the Tehran militants began a series of moves and countermoves, thrusts and parries, with the hostages as pawns.

Carter began by announcing that, since the militants occupying the embassy obviously had the support of and were under the direction of the Ayatollah, the United States would hold the government of Iran directly responsible for the safety of the hostages. This thinly veiled threat of military reprisal, typical of the Carter low-key style, was backed up by the carrier *Midway,* and its supporting task force which was on joint U.S.-British maneuvers in the Arabian Sea and within bombing range of key Iranian military targets. It was underscored, days later, when the carrier *Kitty Hawk* was ordered to the Indian Ocean from the Pacific.

The "students" occupying the embassy immediately announced that any sort of mil-

Showdown with Carter

itary action, or even the hint of it, would result in instant death for all the hostages. Carter followed with an announcement suspending the sale and delivery of $300 million worth of military equipment and spare parts to Iran. From his righteous perch in Qum, the Ayatollah, more popular with his people than ever, looked down on the fray.

It was sometime during the second week that Carter's restrained, methodical handling of the crisis began to have its impact. Americans overwhelming approved of his approach, and the international community found itself completely sympathetic with Washington.

The U.N. Security Council refused to debate charges brought against the United States by Abolhassan Bani-Sadr, the new Iranian Chief of Foreign Affairs. First, the hostages must be freed.

Meanwhile, Americans by the thousands demonstrated spontaneously across the country. Carter ordered the U.S. Immigration and Naturalization Service to start proceedings to deport any Iranian students found to be in this country illegally.

The rhetoric of the confrontation, meanwhile, was heating up. In Iran, the Ayatollah charged that "All western governments are thieves," while another Muslim revolutionary and ayatollah called for a jihad against the United States.

Carter, in a speech before the AFL-CIO National Convention, asserted that "the United States will not yield to international terrorism and blackmail," and that he was simultaneously "trying to protect the honor of our country and the lives of the hostages." The President, perhaps stung by his reputation, was still quite conscious of showing the American people there was a difference between being cautious and being "weak-willed."

If the President had been slow in anticipating events in Iran, now that the crisis was upon him, he showed great skill. When there were hints of an Iranian oil cutoff against the United States, Carter swiftly announced an oil boycott. It was a political risk that the White House overwhelmingly won with the added advantage of being able to excuse, in the name of patriotism, what would have been higher oil prices anyway.

When Iran threatened to withdraw their twelve billion dollars from U.S. banks, Carter declared a "national emergency" and froze their assets, denying them access to their own money. The shock waves of this move were felt around the world, as other governments, particularly the oil producing countries, saw a

Showdown with Carter

dangerous precedent.

Even so, some of the President's strongest support was coming from other Muslim countries who feared that Khomeini's long-range plans might include uprisings of the Shiite Muslim sect in their own countries. Particularly vocal in their condemnation of the radicalism under Khomeini were the leaders of the two largest Sunni Muslim countries, Anwar Sadat of Egypt, and the ruling family of Saudi Arabia.

Suddenly and unexpectedly, the first apparent breakthrough in the stalemate occurred. Foreign Minister Bani-Sadr hinted that some of the hostages, the women and blacks, might be released. This first glimmer of hope in a totally dark situation was almost immediately snuffed out by the militants holding the hostages.

At first, they announced that the statement by Bani-Sadr "had no meaning," and that there would be no release of any hostages until the United States returned the Shah.

This statement was rescinded under an order by Khomeini to release the women because "Islam grants to women a special status" and the blacks because they had "spent ages under American pressure and tyranny."

These actions both encouraged and con-

THE IRAN CRISIS

fused the American public. It appeared there was some progress, but Americans were now confronted by the same dilemma that Washington diplomats had been wrestling with for days. Who ruled in Iran?

Bani-Sadr was assumed to speak for Khomeini and Khomeini was assumed to be the leader. However, the students made it clear that Bani-Sadr did not speak for them, and, when he came under criticism by the students, Khomeini appeared to withdraw his support. The students had acquiesced to a direct order from Khomeini, but was this blind obedience or was it the attraction of the "women and blacks" appeal? Was there anyone in Tehran who could be relied on as the official spokesman? The answer became obvious very soon. It was an emphatic, "No."

While the militants dawdled over the release of some of the hostages, staging a kangaroo press conference with one woman and two black marines for the American television cameras, the most frightening announcement, thus far, was made concerning the rest of the hostages. They would be tried for espionage in the Islamic Revolutionary Courts and "punished in accordance with the severity of their crimes."

This shocking news was confirmed by Kho-

Showdown with Carter

meini, who asserted that the only thing that would halt the trials would be the return of the Shah.

Whatever the outcome was to be, it became apparent that, for all the political, economic, and military power at the disposal of the President of the United States, the hostage card in this frightening game was not in his hands.

The Ayatollah Khomeini gained time. His nation's unemployment had reached twenty-five percent. The Kurds, promised a measure of autonomy, had felt betrayed and were openly calling for separation. The embassy crisis had come at the right time. The "American devils" could henceforth be blamed for any economic crisis or political division.

But there was a limit to the hostage case. Boycotts and sanctions, indeed bullets, may not rattle the angry old mullah, but the Iranian people could not live forever on their enthusiastic anti-Americanism.

However, the consensus, that second week in November, was that U.S. President Jimmy Carter had even less time. He, too, in a serendipitous fashion, had benefited by the tragic events. Politically, he was even stronger. Internationally, America had achieved a stature and sympathy without parallel. She had the 1950-ish affection of Western Europe, the coopera-

THE IRAN CRISIS

tion of many Communist countries; she was, in fact, almost being courted by the Chinese, and remarkably, she was the object of great sympathy by Third Worlders. All of the State Department's elaborate machinery and ingenious plans could not have produced such an effect. But it remained to be seen if the administration could take advantage of the world's mood and achieve anything lasting. Both Carter's political advantage and America's prestige were on the line. Both were thought to be temporary, or maybe even an illusion altogether.

Basking in the sunshine of popularity with their own people, both the Ayatollah and the American President had raised the ante. It would be extremely difficult to secure a compromise. The stalemate could not last forever. Someone now had to lose.

6

Islam Aflame

On Tuesday, November 20, 1979, two hundred armed fanatics took over the sacred mosque in Mecca, Saudi Arabia. The group had entered the forty-acre courtyard at the center of the shrine carrying coffins above their heads, looking much like other funeral marches that come and go.

Mohammed Abdullah al-Utaibah, leader of the band, interrupted the morning call to prayer. Claiming to be the Islamic messiah, Mohammed directed his army to break open the coffins filled with rifles and hand grenades. The fanatics grabbed hostages from among the crowd of 50,000 worshipers and then ran to prearranged points throughout the mammoth shrine.

Saudi Arabia's conservative government,

already skittish over Khomeini and the problems in Iran, immediately cut off all communications with the outside world. Having received a special dispensation from Muslim holy men to do battle in Islam's most sacred shrine, King Khalid ordered in helicopters and armored vehicles.

At the Palais de Congrés in Tunisia, twenty Arab heads of state were meeting when the news from Mecca reached them. The Saudi blackout and the fact that Mohammed Abdullah's gunmen were still fighting and thus could not be positively identified, resulted in a flood of excitement and exaggerated stories.

Persistent rumors that the American CIA was behind the sacrilege floated through the hallways and lounges. The Saudis suspected the unpredictable Gaddafi, radical leader of Libya, who had refused to participate at the summit. Fears that the gunmen in the mosque may be pro-Khomeini Shiites and that the attack may even be the harbinger of a Shiite-Sunni Muslim conflict were beneath the surface, but not referred to publicly.

The next day in Iran, a mysterious radio report linked the attack in Mecca to the CIA and "Zionists." Within twenty-four hours, the news spread throughout the Muslim world. The Ayatollah Khomeini endorsed the radio

Islam Aflame

report that same night, saying that the United States and Israel had staged the whole event.

Hodding Carter at the U.S. State Department called Khomeini's charge an "outright lie," but even as he spoke the Islamic world erupted.

The violence began in Pakistan. At 1:00 P.M. on November 21, angry mobs attacked the U.S. embassy in Islamabad. Two American servicemen were killed before embassy personnel successfully retreated into the vault room. There they waited for the Pakistani Army to rescue them. The rescue never came. Pakistani soldiers watched as the embassy was put to the torch.

Within four hours, the blaze threatened to fry the one hundred embassy personnel alive. When flames erupted inside the red-hot steel, bulletproof room, a calm American official grabbed a fire extinguisher and smothered the blaze.

Deciding they preferred to chance the mobs outside to being cooked in the vault, the one hundred made a dash through a security exit to the roof. Darkness had fallen on Islamabad by then and the mob had receded, content to look on at their handiwork. As enormous flames shot up into the black sky, embassy personnel descended a ladder. They were greeted by

THE IRAN CRISIS

Pakistani soldiers. Convinced that the mob was finished, the army suddenly received orders to "rescue" the Americans after all. It had been seven hours since the embassy had called for help.

At the State Department in Washington, D.C., the map of Asia began to flash trouble spots. The same day mobs had attacked the embassy in Islamabad, Pakistanis had burned American cultural centers in Rawalpindi and Lahore.

On Thursday, November 22, from his headquarters in Qum, Khomeini called on the world's Muslims to join the "struggle between the infidels and Islam." The Ayatollah's fiery speech received worldwide coverage. In Bangladesh, a large crowd demonstrated in front of the American embassy, accusing the CIA of inspiring the attack on the Sacred Mosque in Mecca. That same day, in Izmir, Turkey, angry Muslims broke windows at the U.S. Consulate.

On Friday, the Muslim minority in Calcutta, India, demonstrated. Huge mobs attacked the American and, curiously, the Russian Consulates. Automobiles were set ablaze, but Calcutta's surprisingly efficient, riot-trained police battled furiously, bringing the crowds into submission.

The spontaneous eruption of Islamic passion had a profound effect in most world

Islam Aflame

capitals. In Moscow and New Delhi, governments had to consider the possible impact Khomeini could have on their Muslim minorities. Nerves were tense in Riyadh and Cairo and Rabat where Muslim governments had special relationships with the United States and were being cast by Khomeini radicals as "tools of the West." Every nation had to deal with the emergence of a socio-political force which threatened to upset world equilibrium. To whose advantage, no one could be certain, but the interruption was frightening.

The Islamic awakening had no greater impact than in Washington, D.C. Only days before, Khomeini was thought to have been skillfully isolated. A public opinion index in France showed sixty-four percent agreed that Carter should not return the Shah. Nine European nations denounced the Iranian threat to put the hostages on trial for "spying" and called for their release.

Even the Russians came close to providing support for the U.S. position. Perhaps spurred by concern that trials for the hostages would force the American government into actions which would be detrimental to Soviet interests in the Persian Gulf, Russian radio stations, broadcasting in Farsi and beamed into Iran, called for the hostages to be freed as a "humanitarian gesture."

The threat to try the American diplomats for espionage had triggered an escalation of hostilities between the two countries that seemed to be propelling both toward the edge of the abyss of war and neither seemed to be able to pull back.

The militants holding the hostages pointed to a number of specific charges designed to portray them as spies, rather than diplomats. Working from a definition of "espionage" supplied by Chief Islamic Prosecutor Hassam Gaffarpour, which included even the gathering of information that could be used in any operation against the Islamic community, the militants began pointing to specific events which they claimed fit that rather broad definition.

One of these was a statement made by embassy secretary Joan Walsh that after turning down a request for support and intelligence on events in the country from exiled former Prime Minister Shahpour Bakhtiar, embassy personnel had expressed a desire to maintain communication with him. This was seen by the militants as help from the United States for Bakhtiar's encouragement of separatist movements.

Another charge leveled at embassy personnel was that they were trying to undermine the

Islam Aflame

Iranian economy by flooding it with counterfeit dollars, deutsche marks and Iranian rials that had been found inside the embassy. When Iranian officials admitted that the counterfeit bills had been brought to the U.S. embassy by an Iranian citizen and that the Americans had apparently been engaged in trying to track down the real counterfeiters, the militants dismissed the story.

Obviously, the threat by the students to bring the hostages to trial was designed to bring added pressure on the U.S. government to extradite the deposed Shah. However, the fact that this was an option that was simply not available to the government was recognized even at the highest levels of the Iranian government. The second most visible figure in Iranian government was Abolhassan Bani-Sadr, acting Foreign Minister. In an exceptional bit of insight into the American quandary, Bani-Sadr admitted that the United States, "as a land of free people," could not, in good conscience, turn over the Shah for virtually certain execution, or suffer the humiliation of trading the life of "this sick man" for the lives of fifty hostages.

The threat of bringing the hostages to trial for espionage probably would not have been taken nearly so seriously by Americans, had it

THE IRAN CRISIS

come from practically any other country in the world. Accepted international practice for foreign diplomats accused of spying was simply expulsion. In this case, however, the past record of the Islamic Revolutionary courts led to fears that the hostages might indeed be killed. This fear was heightened by a statement by Chief Prosecutor Gaffarpour that those found guilty of espionage would be shot.

When the threat of espionage trials was made, President Carter responded immediately. The feeling in Washington was that what had been a signal of restraint on the administration's part had been interpreted by the Ayatollah and the militants as cowardice, that the United States was really afraid to retaliate.

Since failure to disabuse them of this notion might lead to further danger for the hostages, Carter authorized a statement to the press that, while the United States "preferred" a peaceful solution, other alternatives were available.

The American President's first public threat of military action was accentuated by a massive naval force ordered into position. Two carrier battle groups, the *Midway* and the *Kitty Hawk*, and a Mideast Naval Task Force steamed into the Persian Gulf. Nearly one hundred fifty warplanes were within striking distance of Iran. In Washington, the Pentagon had decided that U.S. military action would have to be punitive. There still seemed to be no Entebbe-style raid option. Ironically, the Arab world was rattled further by speculation in the U.S. press as to what military options were available. Among those listed was a naval blockade of imported food and exported oil products, bombing of selected military and strategic targets, and, finally, the bombing of the holy city of Qum itself.

If President Carter wanted to get across the message that the United States was prepared for military action, he succeeded. In fact, he succeeded too well. What was intended to be seen as military preparedness was seen instead as anticipated military aggression. Spurred by inflammatory speeches by Khomeini, the Iranian population prepared for what they believed was an imminent invasion in which they may be called to martyrdom for Islam.

Iran's almost hysterical reaction to the U.S. military presence had a couple of explanations. First, Khomeini may have once again seized on an opportunity to rally his people behind him and focus their attention away from their rapidly deteriorating economy and onto the American "infidels."

The Iranian economy was in a state of virtual collapse and had shown signs of further

THE IRAN CRISIS

deterioration as the crisis dragged on. Several food and drug items were in extremely short supply and were being hoarded. Unemployment had risen even more, to approximately 25 percent of the total work force.

A second probable reason for the passionate Iranian reaction to an American military presence was the pitiful state to which Iran's own military had sunk. Under the Shah, Iran's army and air force had been among the best trained and equipped in the world. In the few short months of the ascent of the Ayatollah, that picture had totally changed.

Any and all army leaders who were identified with the Shah had been purged or executed. Fighter planes were practically falling apart due to lack of maintenance and spare parts. It was questionable as to how many, if any, were able to fly. Helicopters and other military hardware had suffered badly from the fact that almost all spare parts were supplied from the United States and that source had been cut off by the government. Discipline and leadership in the army was at such a low ebb that the vaunted Persian Army had been unable to contain Kurdish tribesmen, let alone deal with an outside invasion.

Since Khomeini knew he was not able to respond militarily to the threat of U.S. military

Islam Aflame

action, he may have chosen to escalate the verbal war, where his offensive weapons were at their sharpest. First calling on all Islamic people to join him in a "battle against the infidel," he then taunted the Americans by saying that his people considered martyrdom a great honor and that Jimmy Carter "didn't have the guts" to take military action.

Muslims observing their holy, month-long sacred period of Muharram, as well as the first anniversary of the fall of the Shah, took to the streets. The religious dressed themselves in Muslim burial shrouds and flailed at themselves with chain whips to demonstrate their willingness, and even eagerness, to become martyrs in support of Khomeini. Weeks after the takeover of the embassy, tension in Tehran and the fever of the street mobs were at their highest pitch.

During December's Muharram, month of mourning, Khomeini moved to solidify his power base at home. A new Iranian constitution would give him unlimited lifetime power over the government of Iran. A proposed elected parliament would be totally under the thumb of the Constitutional Protective Council. This council, made up of six Islamic clergy and six devout Muslim laymen, would be appointed by the Fagih, the country's leading clergyman, Khomeini. The "enlightened" new Islamic Revolutionary constitution would replace the corrupt Pahlavi monarchy with a Fagih who would have absolute veto power over all governmental decisions made either by the parliament or the council and who would be designated commander-in-chief of all armed forces. In other times, the Ayatollah's outrageous constitution would have torn the nation asunder but these were not normal times. Every indication was that the document would be overwhelmingly approved without change.

With world news preoccupied with the Islamic demonstrations across the Middle East, on November 20, almost unnoticed, the first thirteen hostages were released by the militants. Obedient to a Khomeini order, all but one black and most of the women were packaged up and sent home. Rationalizing that women had a "special status" in Islam and that blacks had spent too many years already suffering under American "tyranny," Khomeini staged a media event to announce the release of the thirteen.

The obvious political intent of Khomeini's decision and the cynicism with which he used the hostages prompted immediate denouncements. American blacks and women to whom

Islam Aflame

the Ayatollah was apparently appealing found their patriotism and intelligence insulted. American unity tightened another notch.

World reaction was equally unanimous. Many Third Worlders were embarrassed by Khomeini's special treatment for blacks. European nations thought the whole event so crude that it was difficult for them not to condemn it, no matter how reluctant they were to offend Iran and place their own oil imports from that country in jeopardy.

Nevertheless, for the five white women and eight black men, the Ayatollah's failed strategy meant Thanksgiving at home with their families. On Thursday, November 22, the thirteen arrived at Andrews Air Force Base near Washington, D.C. Relatives had been brought there by the State Department. After a subdued welcome by Secretary of State Cyrus Vance, they were treated to a Thanksgiving dinner on the State Department.

The released hostages were reluctant to talk about their ordeal. Some, fearful that the Iranians would carry out Khomeini's threat of trial and death for their remaining colleagues, said nothing. Piecemeal information from the others shed a tale of isolation and inquisition. The daily regimen included the militants' rather simplistic attempts to politically reeducate their captives, sometimes accompanied by personal, physical intimidation.

The hostages were awakened at 7:00 A.M.; meals consisted of Iranian bread and cheese. Most were blindfolded throughout the day; light bulbs burning throughout the night interfered with sleep.

Terry Tedford of San Francisco told reporters she could not have endured "another day." Captain Neal Robinson, USAF, of Houston, Texas, described it as "a very controlled environment. They were our fathers and mothers. We had to ask for everything. We had to ask for sleep."

The most significant result of the release of the thirteen was a worldwide call for the release of those who remained. Seeking to give the Iranian government an excuse to end the crisis, the U.S. State Department continued to search for a new home for Mohammed Pahlavi.

The first week of December, Washington explored the idea of returning the former monarch to his walled Cuernavaca hideaway estate in Mexico. These hopes brightened when the Shah's doctors announced the completion of medical treatment. Mexican Foreign Secretary Jorge Castaneda expressed a "pleasant welcome."

But the expected departure was abruptly

Islam Aflame

aborted when the Mexican government, apparently learning that the Shah's reputed billions were only a myth, suddenly changed its mind and refused reentry.

The Shah was meanwhile whisked to San Antonio, Texas, where he promptly entered the hospital at Lackland Air Force Base for a recuperative stay. Presidential spokesman Jody Powell announced that the United States would assist the former king in making arrangements for a permanent place of residence.

Though the presence of Mohammed Pahlavi posed an enigma to Washington, President Carter reinforced his "never yield to blackmail" stance at a nationally televised press conference. An NBC News-Associated Press poll showed Americans supporting the President's handling of the crisis by a three to one margin. An ABC-Lou Harris poll showed Carter within four points of the once unbeatable Ted Kennedy.

And, yet, parallel to Carter's own political comeback, the Ayatollah's popularity in Iran was greater than ever. During the first week of December, using red ballots to say "no," and the Islamic color of green to say "yes," Iran overwhelmingly approved the new constitution with its *vel ayate faghih* (rule of clergy) clause.

THE IRAN CRISIS

The referendum struck some as too severe. There were suspicions that the Ayatollah had overplayed his hand. Proudly promoted as a "pure" Islamic document, the constitution did indeed offend key Muslim leaders. In Tabriz, one million Turks boycotted the vote and, two days after its adoption, revolted from Qum, declaring support of the moderate Ayatollah Kazem Sharietmadari.

Nevertheless, the legal document legitimized Khomeini's rule. Ordering his Revolutionary militia out of Tabriz and the rebellious northern Azerbaijan province, Khomeini met in Qum with his old rival, Sharietmadari. While major differences remained, the two emerged united as Islamic brothers. "Iran must remain as one before the infidels."

In a national address, Khomeini warned the nation, "Equip yourselves, get military training. Train your friends. America will lose, Islam will win!" The militants at the embassy told reporters, "The United States doesn't realize it is fighting God!"

7

The Missing Hostages

The coming Iranian constitutional vote was upstaged by depressing news for the American government. Foreign Minister Abolhassan Bani-Sadr had been fired. Bani-Sadr, by Iranian standards a moderate, had engineered the release of the thirteen blacks and women, and had openly opposed the trial of the hostages. It was known that the foreign minister was anxiously awaiting his chance to visit the United Nations to "air Iranian grievances." The U.S. State Department had been looking to the visit as a start in a negotiated resolution of the crisis. The Ayatollah's new foreign minister, Sadegh Ghotbzadeh, quickly announced there would be no Iranian pilgrimage to the United Nations.

The emergence of Ghotbzadeh and the fall of Bani-Sadr raised new anxiety over the question

THE IRAN CRISIS

of who, besides the inaccessible Khomeini, would be a reliable representative of the Revolutionary government.

For weeks the Americans had shunned the hostile Ghotbzadeh, at the time only serving in a propaganda role as communications czar. An effort had been made to contact the tall, graying mullah, Seyyed Mohammed Beheshti. Given the clerical nature of the government, Western diplomats had tagged Beheshti, secretary of the Revolutionary Council, as the second power in Iran. The fall of Bani-Sadr closed that door and the Americans were forced to deal with a new man.

Ghotbzadeh, a suave, well-read, forty-three-year-old bachelor, fluent in several languages, was erroneously portrayed in the West as an intellectual lightweight. The antagonism between the new Iranian foreign minister and the Americans could be traced back to the former's earlier time in the States. Exiled by the Shah, Ghotbzadeh had lived in Washington, D.C., until State Department authorities expelled him in 1963. Subsequent travels linked him to a host of radical anti-American forces (such as the Palestine Liberation Organization and the Communist Party).

Critics dismissed him as a political opportunist repeatedly jumping from position to position in furthering his ambitions. One of those switches brought him into contact with Khomeini during the latter's exile in France. Ghotbzadeh claimed to be a faithful disciple of the Ayatollah, rather expediently tracing his support back sixteen years.

Many Iranians were rather dubious about the new foreign minister. Though claiming to be a devout Muslim, the bachelor was not particularly known for an Islamic life style, touring the more poverty-stricken areas of Tehran in his old automobile and hobnobbing with the elite in a Mercedes limousine.

Regardless of contradictions or motives, Ghotbzadeh promised to be a radical voice to carry Khomeini's pro-Islamic/anti-American banner. The new foreign minister had successfully orchestrated the propaganda of the revolution from the beginning. Ruthlessly purging political enemies, initiating strict media censorship, and successfully linking anti-American sentiment with Islamic devotion, Ghotbzadeh appeared to have emerged from the Revolutionary power struggle as Qum's spokesman, if not one of the most powerful shapers of its policy.

The Bani-Sadr/Ghotbzadeh switch led to great American frustration. In his first televised news conference since the embassy takeover,

THE IRAN CRISIS

U.S. President Carter warned of "grave consequences" if any harm came to the hostages. The President's controversial mother, Lillian, campaigning in New Hampshire, told an audience that if she had an extra million dollars, she'd "look for someone to kill" the Ayatollah. The audience cheered.

But America's stubborn and unified face was soon shattered. On December 2, in a television interview in San Francisco, presidential contender Edward Kennedy described the Shah's regime as "one of the most violent" in the history of mankind. Kennedy told of "violations of human rights under the most cruel circumstances to his people."

The Kennedy announcement brought cheers from the streets of Tehran. "Right on, Kennedy" posters began to appear. Ghotbzadeh told reporters that this was the type of self-criticism Iranians were calling for and was a "good sign."

If the American Senator's comments had appeal in Iran, they could not have come at a more inappropriate time for his own domestic political ambitions. Kennedy was called the "Toast of Iran" in the headlines of the *New York Post*. Editors of the *Washington Post*, considered by some as hostile to the Carter administration, pointedly suggested that if the Massachusetts Senator believed the Shah's

The Missing Hostages

government to be corrupt he should have criticized it in his 1975 visit to Iran.

In actuality, Ted Kennedy had done just that. During his visit in May of that year, he had discouraged the King's "military mania." As his brother, John F. Kennedy, had done before him, Ted had warned of the drain of heavy arms expenditures and the problem it posed for the economic progress of the country. In a highly publicized visit with students at the University of Tehran, Kennedy had asked, "How many people around this table can tell me what your government is spending on arms?" To the eternal enmity of the Shah, Kennedy had publicly given the budgetary figures, secret stuff in Iran's censored pre-Revolutionary society. The students had been scandalized.

But it was the Shah who had come out best in the latest Pahlavi-Kennedy episode. Senator Ted Kennedy, whose comments had come in response to a Ronald Reagan suggestion for a permanent U.S. asylum for Mohammed Pahlavi, saw his political fortunes dive. For the first time, presidential preference polls showed Jimmy Carter leading his Democratic challenger.

On the frosty morning of December 15, Americans awoke to find the Shah gone. For weeks, ever since the Mexican government had denied him re-entry into the country, there had been speculation about his future. Egypt had issued a formal invitation, but it was thought that the deposed ruler's presence would be much too dangerous for Sadat and perhaps cause serious repercussions with other Arab countries. State Department officials flatly stated that the man would not be "put out to sea in a rowboat," although allowing him to stay in the United States seemed nearly as dangerous as sending him to Egypt

Though the Shah had previously ruled out going to Panama and the Bahamas, President Carter's Chief of Staff, Hamilton Jordan, was secretly sent to visit Panamanian strong man, Omar Torrijos Herrara. The presidential aide and Torrijos had become friends and "drinking buddies" during the Panama Canal Treaty negotiations and, after a late-night diplomatic talk, Torrijos officially extended the invitation to the Shah.

Early Saturday morning, Mohammed Reza Pahlavi and his family were secretly rushed to an air force jet, flown to Panama, and then, sixty miles further southeast in the blue Pacific, to the tiny island of Contadora. The Americans had finally succeeded. The Shah was gone and the way seemed open to talk with Iran about

The Missing Hostages

the hostages.

The militants in Tehran, however, shrugged off the gesture. "It will make no difference," they said. "We want the Shah."

Only days later, in an event staged for NBC television, Western reporters were given access to one of the hostages, Marine Corporal William Gallegos. The controversial show began with an uncensored, unedited statement from a militant spokeswoman. Once again the Americans were reminded of the rules. The hostages would be released when and if the Shah was returned to Iran. The move to Panama was unacceptable.

Corporal Gallegos, in his appearance before television cameras, answered questions with painful and martial deliberation. He satisfied the predictions of some psychiatrists and students of kidnapping situations by expressing sympathy for his captors' goal of pursuing the Shah's past crimes, but similarly, the marine revealed a defiance that belied rumors of effective brainwashing. Assuring the nation that "nobody's been mistreated," Gallegos nonetheless admitted he could not speak to other hostages and that there were some twenty whom he had not seen.

Within the week, the Western world learned from Iranian news sources that the condition of the hostages was not as idyllic as Gallegos had portrayed. The daily schedule had been stepped up. Now rising at 6:30 A.M. for brief exercise, twice a week allowed shower privileges (with no clothing changes), the captives were at all other times kept seated, their hands bound, their feet bare. Use of toilet facilities required special permission. Periodic cigarette breaks allowed by the jailers were reported to have prompted nonsmokers to pick up the habit as a diversion and as an excuse to have their hands untied. (In Islamic fashion, men were allowed more cigarettes than women.) The hostages were permitted only to talk to the guards. At ten in the evening, they were allowed to sleep on mattresses, but slumber was frequently broken by middle-of-the-night interrogation sessions, sometimes with threats.

The tensions and anxieties on Gallegos's face, and the tears on the cheeks of his parents watching from Pueblo, Colorado, had renewed the intense American vigil for their compatriots. Trees and festive lights were lighted as usual in preparation for the holidays, but Americans were quieter, more pensive this Christmas. An ABC television late-night update, *The Iran Crisis*, became a favorite show. Bumper stickers began to appear, "Release the hostages." Newspaper mastheads began to count the days of the captivity.

The Missing Hostages

Aside from reviving American passions and concern for the fate of the hostages, the controversial Gallegos interview prompted a reappraisal of the media role in the crisis. Journalists and television news personalities depicting themselves in their own reports as reluctant, but heroic, mediators and diplomats began to come under great scrutiny by the U.S. State Department. Could the crisis be resolved quicker without the press?

The news coverage seemed to be motivated more toward getting attention than by anger towards the hostages. The students became actors on cue when the camera lights blinked.

American newsmen walked the streets of Tehran quite safely despite Iran radio's endless, anti-American barrage. The hostages inside the embassy were told they were bound for their own safety; if they were to escape, the shrieking mob outside would tear them limb from limb simply because they were Americans. Yet, outside, U.S. newsmen were recognized as celebrities.

Just weeks before, the crowds had seethed with anger against the reporters and the Ayatollah considered expelling the "infidel" newsmen. By the second week of December, the crowd had learned to shout on cue. In fact, some seasoned reporters were shocked at Iranians who silently shook fists when only a camera was trained on them, but suddenly became quite verbal when a microphone was offered.

Even as the Western media, in an embarrassing fit of self-importance, held itself out as the key to resolving the stalemate and Carter's only link to the Iranians, secret talks had indeed begun between Washington and Qum. The pressures of the world community, the impact of a unanimous U.N. Security Council resolution calling for the release of the American diplomats, and most ominously, the proposed economic sanctions against Iran began to bear down on the radical and ostensibly ascetic leaders of the Revolutionary Council.

On December 13, Iranian Foreign Minister Sadegh Ghotbzadeh, in a clever appeal to the American press and its claim as mediator, sent the Carter administration a message. (The same message was relayed through U.S. Chargé d'Affaires Bruce Laingen.) "An American investigation of the Shah's crimes," Ghotbzadeh said, "would be a positive step" toward resolving the crisis. The hostages might be released without trial.

Like all doors out of the Iranian crisis, this one slammed shut before Washington had time to think about it. On the same day of the Ghotbzadeh announcement, three Khomeini

The Missing Hostages

associates were gunned down in Tehran. Mohammed Mofateh, head of Tehran's School of Theology and a close Khomeini friend, was among those slain. Seventy-nine-year-old Ayatollah Khomeini could not resist the opportunity to rouse the faithful. The American CIA was tagged as the assassin, and hysterical mobs surged back into Iranian streets. The Ayatollah Khalkhali, who had presided over Revolutionary Courts which had sentenced 620 to death, announced that Iranian agents had been dispatched to kill the Shah.

At the American embassy, the militants denounced Ghotbzadeh's gesture of possible release, warning that the foreign minister was "going over the limit in remarks about the spies and their trials." Ghotbzadeh was described as "out of tune with the revolution."

But, contrary to the often undermined announcements of his predecessor, Bani-Sadr, the new foreign minister had prepared the ground beneath him. The next day, with mobs in the streets of Qum carrying the caskets of the slain martyrs and chanting, "Death-to-Car-ter," Ghotbzadeh reiterated that his December 18 announcement accurately reflected the view of the Revolutionary Council.

Secretary Seyyed Beheshti confirmed Ghotbzadeh's standing in his controversy with the embassy militants. "The last decision should be taken by the Revolutionary Council and the Imam," Beheshti announced. "The ideas of our students and people will be considered in these decisions." The students answered by promising once again to obey only Khomeini.

Just as Muslim holy days had aroused Iran, the approaching Christmas celebration was looming as an important deadline to Americans. The U.S. State Department exerted every pressure to bring about a diplomatic solution. Appealing to the World Court in the Hague, the Americans succeeded in forcing an emergency session with judges flying in from across the globe to hear the case.

Radio disc jockeys began a campaign for Christmas cards, obtaining permission from Ghotbzadeh to allow the mail through. The militants shrugged off the effort. "If they want Christmas cards, they can have them. We don't mind. It's not important."

Department stores erected huge signs, "Send a Christmas Card to the Hostages!" Some cards were given away, the stores asking only that the senders pay for the postage to Taleghani Street. A long, sixty-foot scroll was signed by hundreds of people, rolled up, and mailed to the embassy. Post offices were deluged; 151,000 pieces of mail per day went through John F.

The Missing Hostages

Kennedy Airport alone. Eventually, over 1.1 million cards flooded the embassy in Tehran. After days of the downpour, the militants began to angrily seize the hundreds of mailbags, jerking them through the embassy gates.

Hope was strong that a few of the hostages might be freed as a symbolic Christmas gift, perhaps a couple of the men with severe health problems, or maybe the two women who had been detained after all the others had come home.

On December 22, by invitation of the Ayatollah, three American clergymen were invited to the embassy to celebrate holy services with the hostages. For the first time since November 5, the captives would be seen personally by their fellow countrymen.

On Christmas Eve, Foreign Minister Ghotbzadeh announced that some hostages would be released later in the day by order of the Ayatollah, but this time, the confident foreign minister lost in his showdown with the militants. The message from Taleghani Street was that no hostages would be released until the Shah was returned.

Prayers were whispered all over the United States. In Albany, New York, a replica of the Liberty Bell rang out fifty times, its golden cord swung in remembrance of the fifty. A candle-

THE IRAN CRISIS

light vigil in Boston was held with children of hostage, William Keough, in attendance. In another Boston church service, released hostage Marine Corporal Wesley Williams lit fifty candles for his compatriots left behind. White armbands, given out by a local radio station to be worn in honor of the hostages, were gone in a matter of hours. American flags were sold out in stores all over the country. In Washington, President Carter threw a switch, lighting only a lonely star atop the otherwise dark national Christmas tree. In an impassioned voice, the President declared it would remain dark till "our hostages come home."

In Tehran, the Reverend William Sloane Coffin played "Silent Night" on a piano in the American embassy, his full throat overshadowing the bewildered voices of the hostages.

On television, a few days later, the world watched as the Iranian television cameras captured the sight of the hostages moving through the doors into the bright television lights to meet in small groups with the Ayatollah-approved American ministers. The hostages appeared disconcerted and detached. Some sat sullenly on the sofas, making no effort to join in the singing and the worship. Even so, relatives in America rejoiced tearfully as they recognized the stern faces of their husbands and children.

The Missing Hostages

On their return from Tehran, the three clergymen, the Reverends Coffin, Howard and Gumbleton flew directly to the U.S. State Department to meet with officials and the captives' families, bearing intimate messages from the hostages. The ministers reported the hostages to be "bearing up well" and that they had been "moved to tears" by the concern of the country.

The Coffin-Howard-Gumbleton visit prompted a new mystery in the hostage crisis. The pastors, memorizing carefully all they had seen, could only account for forty-three hostages. Where were the other seven? The embassy militants insisted that some had refused to go to the Christmas services "on their own accord," but that statement was discounted in most circles. Some suggested the militant students were punishing seven of their most defiant captives.

Some missing Americans were indeed in Tehran, but not in the hands of the students. Secreted at the home of the Canadian Ambassador to Iran, Kenneth Taylor, several Americans who had escaped the compound on that gray day of November 4 nervously prayed that the inquiry into the whereabouts of the "missing" hostages would subside. Only a handful of intelligence agents and two heads of state knew where they were.

For a few days, the mystery intrigued some journalists who didn't like their stories to have loose ends. Kim King, of Clatskanie, Oregon, notified the press that he had fled the embassy on that very day of November 4 and that he had personally seen other Americans, including one woman and two marines, leaving the back door of a building. The story received little attention and, finally, to the relief of the few American diplomats hiding in Taylor's home and elsewhere across Tehran, the whole question was dropped.

In Krakow, Missouri, Virgil and Toni Sickmann received a letter on December 26 from their son, Marine Sgt. Rodney "Rocky" Sickmann. The letter, dated December 11, charged his family to remain courageous in the face of their heartache. "If I remember right from all the past Christmases and New Years," he wrote, "there wasn't nothing [sic] that could bring a sad face into the house, meaning there better not be any sad faces this year."

Halfway across the world, on the tiny island of Contadora, the object of all the hatred and conflict, Mohammed Reza Pahlavi, was celebrating Christmas vacation with his family,

The Missing Hostages

including his children excused from their American schools for the holidays. A very thin, debilitated Shah strolled slowly over the lush, green lawns. Palm fronds swayed slowly in the humid breeze. The King's checkered, long-sleeved, buttoned-to-the-neck shirt was incongruous in the sweltering heat and was stained dark with perspiration.

Security was tight. Situated just off the beach were Panamanian gunboats and anti-aircraft guns. Wherever the King walked, ten crack security guards followed, and, behind them, a red automobile filled with even more guards. German shepherds circled the Shah's villa.

From Qum, the hanging judge, Khalkhali, had issued bizarre orders to the Fedeyeen of Islam. Kill the Shah, and the children, and the Shahbanou, too, unless she, herself, killed her husband and thus avenged the people. To add greed to the incentives of "Islamic justice" and Iranian patriotism, Khalkhali offered a $100,000 reward to the successful assassin.

And so, beautiful tropical island that it was, Contadora was still a prison, the Shah was at his Ghars, his Elba, his exile. The six-room stucco villa, laid in a setting of swaying palms and deep sapphire sea, was no match for the sumptuous palaces of Tehran.

THE IRAN CRISIS

Farah Diba, the young, spirited coed who, years before, had turned the eyes and the mind of her King, was as defiant as ever. Adjusting to the humiliation, she carefully supervised the preparation of her husband's food, cautioning the chef against spicy dishes. What was left of the royal gall bladder could not take much more. Like his fierce Cossack father before him, the Shah was reduced to simple peasant food.

Faraway, in the palaces of Iran, the Shah's solid gold telephone and a thousand other intimate and personal symbols of his reign lay exactly where he had left them, displayed for the public as evidence of royal corruption. The fireplaces were cold and the huge rooms usually empty, and, yet, visitors came away with the eerie feeling that Mohammed Pahlavi was only away for a short visit. How long could Khomeini last? How long could Iran sustain the madness?

8

The Invasion of Afghanistan

On December 27, 1979, under the pretext of "defending a nation from outside forces," Russian troops invaded Afghanistan. That same day in Kabul, the independent, uncontrollable President Itafizullah Amin was murdered and a new Afghan leader was flown in from Czechoslovakia to take over. With Russian jets now only minutes from the Persian Gulf, the crisis in neighboring Iran took on a new dimension. While the Soviet move seemed to dwarf the whole issue of the hostages, and consequently much of Washington was now preoccupied with an American response to the Soviets, the resolution of differences with Iran became ever more urgent.

Like most events, when viewed retrospectively, the Russian intervention in Afghanistan had followed predictable steps. In April of 1978, Marxists had seized power but had been struggling ever since to hold their grip. Rebelling against "godless, atheistic Communism," Muslim mountain tribes had harassed Kabul and openly fought the army.

Three Afghan presidents had been overthrown, two of them murdered along with their families, as successive Communist regimes tried to deal with the volatile kingdom. In September, 1979, Itafizullah Amin emerged from a bloody coup as the Afghan strong man. The government tried to develop a measure of stability under Amin even at Moscow's expense. It was a dangerous business.

President Noor Taraki, Amin's predecessor, had been the Kremlin favorite. Only days before his fall, Taraki had met with Brezhnev in a highly visible Moscow summit. The Soviet Communist Party Chief had encouraged Taraki to eliminate his rival, Amin, and thus consolidate power. But before the month was out, Amin himself had seized the initiative, and Taraki was eliminated instead. Succeeding to the presidency, Amin moved to secure his office. On October 6, he ordered Soviet Ambassador Pusanov out of the country on charges of conspiring against his regime.

The Invasion of Afghanistan

Amin's move evidently threw KGB plans off balance and allowed his regime to survive another two months. But it was a fatal decision. Whatever qualms the Kremlin had over toppling their own ally were now gone.

Meanwhile, taking its cue from the Communist governments before it, the new Kabul regime launched its own army purge. Defections to the Muslim rebels increased by tens of thousands, some soldiers taking their trucks and rocket launchers with them. An army of 100,000 Afghans was cut in two. The Russians found themselves supporting the very Afghan regime with whom they were quarreling. Amin's Russian force of 7,000 men, with Soviet pilots and MIG 21 fighters, temporarily held rebels in check.

The final Soviet decision to invade Afghanistan came in the third week of November. With the whole Islamic world momentarily aflame, with the Amin regime tottering, and the prospect of a hostile anti-Communist Islamic front stretching across her borders from Turkey to Pakistan, Russia began to see the move as her only choice. Either she would invade with massive forces or eventually the Muslims would weary any Marxist government in Kabul and take power.

The more the Kremlin studied the idea, the

more seductive it must have become. The whole idea was wrought with opportunities. A move into Afghanistan would pull South Asia inside out. In India, newly returned to power, pro-Soviet Indira Gandhi faced the same dangers of isolation she had felt in the brief Pakistani war. On one side was a hostile People's Republic of China. On the other was an American-supplied Pakistan. A Russian move into Kabul would suddenly isolate the corrupt and unstable Pakistani government instead.

An invasion into Afghanistan put the Soviets ever closer to their long-lived ambition of a warm water port. Their jets would be within easy striking distance of the Hormuz Straits and Saudi Arabian oil. Their armies would be in a strategic position to exploit the unpredictable events in Iran. Even their presence nearby could possibly effect a much needed zone of control in the oil rich region of the Persian Gulf. Without leaving Afghanistan, the Soviets could extend a tough political and diplomatic offensive in the region.

Based on previous encounters with the Democratic administration, the Soviets could expect a moral lecture from Washington but little else. During the much touted "Cuban crisis," Carter had been accused of rhetorically declaring the situation "intolerable" and then,

The Invasion of Afghanistan

without the smallest inconvenience to signal disapproval to the Soviets, had dropped the issue. The very day following his tough speech on Cuba, Carter had approved the grain sale to the Russians.

The possibility of Olympic boycotts, or a grain embargo, or even any response at all, seemed remote. The administration had not been stirred by Russian and Cuban intervention in Ethiopia, or South Yemen, or anywhere else. When the Soviets had allowed Cambodian President Hang Samrin to systematically starve the Chinese-backed Khmer people, a crime of Hitlerian dimensions, Carter complained loudly but did not even hint at any kind of punitive response, such as reconsidering SALT II, or tightening control of computer exports, or even recalling a U.S. Ambassador for consultation.

If Carter, who had repeatedly promised not to use grain as a weapon anyway, would not use it over Cuba, the Russians may have felt confident on the eve of the important Iowa presidential caucus in the heart of American farmland, that the President would not play that card now over Afghanistan.

The Russians appeared to have nothing to lose. SALT II was stalled in the U.S. Senate, with its prospects slim. A move into Afghanistan could be justified as an internal Soviet affair. Russian allies and Third Worlders would be impressed by the contrast between Washington's helplessness before Iran, and Moscow's decisions in her own crisis with Iran's next-door neighbor. The mobs in Tehran, obsessed with their anti-Americanism, would be looking the other way.

There was another extremely ironic and complex theory of Russian thinking. It was no secret that the Kremlin held great contempt for the American President. Complaining he was naive, confusing and inconsistent, the Politburo sometimes tried to give the impression that its aggression in the world was taken reluctantly and was even distasteful to them, a policy which they insinuated the Carter administration had invited. According to this theory, the invasion of Afghanistan was thought to be the final blow to a president whose style irritated them. Portrayed as a weak leader, the theory went, Carter would lose reelection. The fact that this extraordinary theory was popular in Washington demonstrated that some of Carter's critics were certainly more naive than they thought the President to be.

On December 28, Jimmy Carter, using the emergency hot line, telephoned Soviet Chief Leonid Brezhnev. The conversation could well

The Invasion of Afghanistan

be the most significant exchange of the Carter White House years. The U.S. President demanded the withdrawal of Soviet troops. Brezhnev, perhaps caught off guard and certainly not yet rehearsed as an apologist for the invasion, held to a rather weak argument of intervention to protect the Islam nation from "outsiders" which, White House aides declared later, they both knew to be false.

The awkward conversation had a devastating effect on the American President. Already stung by an image of weakness, Carter aides leaked to the press that Brezhnev's clumsy and unimpressive explanation was the final insult. Had the Soviet leader taken pains to assure Carter that Moscow did not view it as a violation of Russian zones of control and that the State Department and White House warnings against the move were misunderstood; had Brezhnev attempted any kind of open discussion at all, Carter's extraordinary patience just might have held for a day or so. Or so the line went.

Carter announced to newsmen that he had learned more about the nature of the Soviet Union in the last few days than he had in the previous years. The image of a naive President, only now realizing the cynicism and deception of Moscow, could have been a costly political error. It surely ranked with 1968 presidential candidate George Romney's self-destructive metaphorical reference to being "brainwashed" about Vietnam. In the already news-glutted, highly eventful week, it passed by.

Gathering aides and Cabinet officials, the U.S. President considered the range of punitive options at his disposal. A grain embargo against the Soviets was discussed, but the President was warned that polls showed Americans disapproving of the use of grain as a weapon. The decision would be politically disastrous in Iowa, where the President had only recently moved ahead of Kennedy in the public opinion index of voters. There was much question as to how effective an embargo would be anyway. American balance of payments would suffer, farmers would suffer, and the boycott would be difficult to enforce since the grain could get to the Russians through third parties.

A ban on the export of computer technology, though not as unpopular with Americans as a grain embargo, might not punish the Soviets at all. The French would fill the vacuum, selling the Russians whatever they needed and perhaps strengthening a much feared European-Soviet condominium as a counter to American-Chinese rapprochement.

The boycott of the Olympics was politically

The Invasion of Afghanistan

unpredictable and thus risky. A quick survey showed Americans would favor the boycott but it was doubtful this was a deeply held conviction that would survive the heat of the day and television stories of disheartened athletes. Carter could go down in history as the man who destroyed the Games, idealistically the planet's only apolitical cooperative event. A Carter aide brought up the NBC network and its potential loss. NBC had employed rather ruthless tactics to win the Olympic coverage in the first place. The network could turn nasty.

The hours of consultation ended. Washington buzzed with rumors as to which option, if any, the President would use. When the time for the announcement came, Jimmy Carter chose all three. In January, viewed as a man who put the country above his own political fortunes, Carter trounced his political rival in the Iowa caucuses.

To American critics, the evolution of a definitive Carter administration foreign policy had been a long and costly journey. The very week of the Afghan invasion, former Secretary of State Henry Kissinger warned that Carter's failure to develop a consistency with his Soviet counterparts was leading to a major confrontation. By failing to make the Soviets pay a price for their military adventures in Africa and elsewhere, the United States was inviting the Russians to continue.

Some accused the administration of only reacting in world events, not anticipating nor providing leadership. It was ironically the very criticism Zbigniew Brzezinski had thrown at the Ford-Kissinger White House when Brzezinski called for "architecture," not "acrobatics." Now, in the last year of the first term of his administration, Carter and his State Department found themselves finally employing the very Nixon-Kissinger-conceived "linkage concepts" they had ridiculed in their 1976 election campaign. All Soviet activities must be taken in context. When Moscow violated American interests in one area, she could expect to pay for it in another.

In Washington, armchair diplomats smiled with condescension at the nation which now enthusiastically supported their President. Hadn't Carter prompted the crisis in the first place? But politicians watched with amazement. The President's resurgence in the polls was the greatest and quickest leap in the history of poll taking. If, indeed, the administration's critics were right, if the President was only reaping what he himself had sown, it only

The Invasion of Afghanistan

accentuated his talent to turn the crisis into an advantage.

Whatever the Carter administration may have lacked in comparison to the Nixon-Kissinger-coordinated, long-range strategy, it had shown itself to be quite spectacular at tactical matters which it isolated. As exemplified in the extraordinary Camp David talks, when this President concentrated his prodigious and strong will on any problem, he seemed capable of solving it.

Boycotts notwithstanding, the most effective weapon Carter used against the Soviets was that very political talent and skill which had made him turn what critics said was a liability into an asset.

Only days after Carter's announced "tough stand" against the Russians, a leaked CIA study showed that oil production in the Soviet Union would drop to ten million barrels per day by 1985. The complex and convincing CIA study forecast a serious economic and military crisis for the Russians. The theory that the move into Afghanistan was only a step toward the Persian Gulf became a widespread fear.

The situation looked frightening. There was a very real danger of Iranian or Pakistani separatists appealing for Soviet help to break away from their governments in Tehran or

THE IRAN CRISIS

Islamabad. Baluchistan, which boasted a warm water port, was a possible candidate. Baluchis lived on both sides of the Iranian-Pakistani border and had been agitating for autonomy.

The United States Armed Forces had declined steadily under Nixon and Ford who faced a hostile Congress and were burdened by a massive payroll for the huge American Army in Vietnam, preventing expenditures on the much needed upgrading of weapons. The new Democratic administration had canceled the B-1 bomber, the MX missile program, the neutron bomb, and ignored an urgent appeal for new ships. Carter now announced a five percent increase in the military budget, but any American recovery was thought to be five years off.

Responding to a carefully painted Carter picture of the Afghan crisis, world capitals responded. In the United Nations, 104 countries condemned the Soviet invasion and, in Islamabad, the Conference of Muslim Nations issued a strong anti-Russian statement.

If the Russians were only settling an internal affair, they had erred badly, alienating much of the Third World whose relationship they had carefully cultivated for a decade. If, indeed, the Afghan invasion was only a prelude to further designs, the Soviets had lost any hope of sur-

The Invasion of Afghanistan

prise or of a subtle political move to power in an adjacent country. A KGB-contrived coup d'état or an unconvincing Soviet excuse for invasion wouldn't work and might mean a world united and aroused against blatant Soviet aggression. Sufficiently excited by what critics said was Carter's overreaction to the invasion, the world was watching closely.

And, so, the President of the United States, using his consummate political skills, which, in the international arena, are dignified with the label "statesmanship," threatened to isolate the acknowledged most powerful nation on earth. The Soviets had not found themselves in such a position since the outbreak of hostilities in Korea. The President, only recently scorned by the Russians, earlier criticized by West German and French allies, assaulted by foreign policy critics at home, had maneuvered into an extraordinary position. More united at home and popular abroad than at any time since 1960, America was in a position much stronger than her number of ICBMs showed.

There was one last bizarre wrinkle to Carter's performance in the whole Afghan affair. It dealt with the American President's religious tradition. While Shiite Muslims had seen the mystery of the twelfth Imam revived by Kho-

THE IRAN CRISIS

meini and the Iran crisis, orthodox Jews and Carter-style born-again Christians were now haunted by some ancient legends of their own.

In the sixth century B.C., a Jewish prophet, Ezekiel, had warned of a devastating pre-Armageddon battle in the Middle East. The legend spun a terrifying tale of a mysterious invader from the North named Magog, who, with a rather odd assortment of far-flung allies, would trigger a war that would endanger the world. The "good guys" would win in Ezekiel's story. Israel and her "powerful" ally would destroy eighty percent of the enemy's army.

The Ezekiel prophecy had always been riddled with problems. Eighteenth-century scholars identified the tribes of Magog as the ancestors of the Russian people, and with the ancient tribal names of Moscow and Tubalsk actually mentioned in the same context, the identity seemed unavoidable. The problem was that eighteenth-century Russia held little terror for the world; it certainly posed no threat to Israel which at the time did not even exist. The likelihood that Ethiopia, Libya, Persia and what is today modern Turkey would be the allies of Magog, as the ancient Ezekiel prophetic legend held, seemed logistically, militarily and politically stupid.

But the ancient prophecy retained its fasci-

The Invasion of Afghanistan

ination to theologians and secularists alike. Nineteenth-century philosophers warned that a new industrial age could produce the weapons of war that could make such destruction possible. Dean M'Neil, an Angelican theologian whose works were published in the 1830s, insisted against all probability that Israel would indeed again become a state, and Russia, backward nation that it was, would someday invade the Middle East and be the terrible force that would bring the world to the brink of Armageddon.

In the twentieth century, with each absurd element coming together one by one—the emergence of Russia, the advent of nuclear weapons, the return of Israel—the prophetic legend suddenly leaked out of the seminaries and synagogues. In 1968, a contemporary interpretation, *The Late, Great Planet Earth,* sold millions of copies and, in the 1970s, when Marxist revolutionaries took power in Libya and Ethiopia, only Persia and Turkey remained as unlikely allies of Magog's terrible adventure.

And so it was that the suddenly anti-Zionist Khomeini government, the invasion of Afghanistan, and the CIA report of an acute Soviet oil shortage brought evangelical Christians and orthodox Jews to their feet. This looked like "it."

THE IRAN CRISIS

Of course, this whole fascinating piece of scriptural mysticism has little significance for a secular history of the modern Iran crisis except for the extraordinarily ironic fact that Jimmy Carter, President of the United States, was indeed an evangelical Christian himself and had thus, even as a child, been exposed to fiery Baptist sermons depicting the Soviet's descent into the Middle East. Ezekiel promised Israel that she would be saved by an ally who would be granted by God a "powerful sword." Now, seven thousand years after Ezekiel's incredible description, one of the ancient prophet's own students sat in the Oval Office or jogged across the White House lawn, while an aide, carrying a little black briefcase, hovered nearby like a terrible angel. In the briefcase were the buttons that could plunge the world into hell. An Israeli ally pitted against a Russian army did indeed have "a powerful sword."

During a March 7 foreign policy briefing in the East Room of the White House, National Security Advisor Zbigniew Brzezinski was asked three times about the use of nuclear weapons.

The author, who was himself a participant in the briefing, asked Brzezinski specifically how the United States would stop a Soviet move into the Middle East. Brzezinski suggested that

The Invasion of Afghanistan

the United States could, "One, meet it on its own terms. Two, escalate horizontally, that is to say, use tactics of our own at a time and place of our choosing. And, three, escalate vertically."

When pressed for the American position on a nuclear first strike if conventional weapons failed to contain the Soviets, Brzezinski announced to the astonished participants in the East Room that "We retain that option. If our vital interests are involved, we will react and react effectively." It was the only statement in the comments of either Carter or Brzezinski that was applauded that day. The seven-thousand-year-old mystical warnings of ancient Ezekiel and the months-old prophecies of a modern Jewish statesman, Henry Kissinger, seemed to dovetail frighteningly.

During the last few days of 1979, mobs in Tehran suddenly turned on the Soviet embassy. Chanting "Death to Russia," the crowds were temporarily turned back by Revolutionary guards. The Ayatollah Khomeini stubbornly refused to condemn his Russian friends, but other members of the Revolutionary Council, slowly realizing the threat of the Soviet army now massing on its border, issued a careful denouncement, pledging to support Muslim fighters in Afghanistan.

THE IRAN CRISIS

In Washington, D.C., U.S. officials speaking through their secret pipeline to Qum, continued to stress the Soviet danger and the need to resolve Iranian-American differences.

At the United Nations in New York City, General Secretary Kurt Waldheim received the signal he was looking for. His widely anticipated trip to Iran was on. For the first time in the escalating crisis, there appeared to be some movement toward a solution.

9

The Canadian Caper

On January 2, 1980, the U.N. Secretary-General's helicopter circled the Behest Zahra Cemetery. Waldheim carried wreaths in Iran's national colors to lay at the tombs of patriots killed during the revolution against the Shah. As soon as the helicopter landed, it was met by hundreds of angry demonstrators and alleged victims of the Shah's regime, screaming, "Neither compromise nor surrender! Deliver the Shah!" The fury of the demonstration rose as the crowd began to close in on the diplomat. Scurrying to the relative safety of a nearby bulletproof automobile, Waldheim had urgently ordered the driver, "Go! Go!", his face ashen and visibly shaken.

But an hour away, in a large building that once served as an extravagant officers' club for the Shah's elite, the Secretary-General was confronted with the same scene. Invited by the Khomeini government, those maimed and tortured in Mohammed Pahlavi's prison had come to offer their fingerless hands and blind eyes as evidence of the Shah's crimes.

Waldheim gazed out over them in disbelief, his wide, patrician forehead and lips totally impassive, frozen with years of practice in the highest echelons of diplomacy. Only his eyes, darting from face to face, betrayed compassion for the victims—victims, not only of the Shah's apparent strong-arm tactics, but also of a current government's insatiable thirst for propaganda. None of his vast experience could have prepared him for this. "Madness," his tired eyes seemed to be saying, "utter madness!"

The mob screamed at him, waving dull pink plastic legs and glass eyes. One man, pressing close to the Secretary-General, lifted his tiny five-year-old son, whose arms had allegedly been cut off in an effort to extract a confession from his older brother. Waldheim, almost overwhelmed by the confusing emotions whirling about him, lifted the child into his arms and held him gently.

The hysterical scenes portrayed on television throughout the world gave rise to a general consensus that the U.N. mission had failed.

The Canadian Caper

The government in Iran seemed beyond reason. An African ambassador to the United Nations said the nation was even unable to conduct a diplomatic conversation.

It had been considered a long shot at best. Many of the Secretary-General's colleagues had warned that a failure could damage his prestige and that success was unlikely. Waldheim had left New York on December 31. Only hours later, the United Nations passed a resolution giving him seven days to achieve a breakthrough. If unsuccessful, debate would begin immediately on economic sanctions against Iran. Waldheim's early departure was meant to convince Tehran that the mission was not contrived by pressure from the United States. But the Secretary-General's journey had only begun when the State Department betrayed him. When a reporter questioned whether the trip was the result of a U.S. suggestion, Secretary of State Cyrus Vance answered blithely, "I think it is, and I'm delighted."

And so, the diplomat's hope of an impartial visit, free of outside pressure, was dashed. The Iranian government, picking up on Vance's statement, and remembering Waldheim's courteous greeting to the Shah in earlier years, responded to the visit with coldness. The Revolutionary Council denied that the U.N. Chief

THE IRAN CRISIS

had been invited by any government official. The old Ayatollah had contemptuously refused to see him, stating flatly, "I do not trust this man."

The students at the embassy had turned their backs, the gates remaining locked to him. "Waldheim is not trustworthy," they announced. "He has proved that he is in the service of the superpowers." A picture of the Secretary-General kissing the hand of Princess Ashraf was smeared all over Tehran newspapers, and the television screens coupled him with gory pictures of alleged SAVAK victims.

On New Year's Day, the third holiday spent in captivity by the American hostages, Waldheim had met with Foreign Minister Ghotbzadeh. The three-hour meeting appeared to be a futile encounter with the diplomat listening to yet another diatribe, berating the United Nations for ignoring the Shah's "atrocities" until goaded into it because of the crisis. Ghotbzadeh ominously reiterated a warning that the hostages would be tried as spies if economic sanctions were voted by the United Nation.

The Secretary-General was viewed as painfully and patiently accepting his own captivity in what amounted to another Iranian government performance. ABC News correspondent,

Barry Dunsmore referred to Waldheim's "embarrassing, if not abortive, mission."

But the Secretary-General's trip to Tehran was not as empty as it seemed. The integrity and objectivity of the U.N. Chief had its impact on Iranians who had dismissed the international organization they called the "tool of the superpowers."

The Secretary of the Revolutionary Council, Ayatollah Mohammed Beheshti, suggested that Waldheim's fact-finding mission might lead to "a wise solution to the present crisis."

Soon after Waldheim's trip, secret negotiations began in Paris between Assistant Secretary of State for Near East Affairs, Hal Saunders, and lawyers once retained by the Iranian Foreign Minister, Sadegh Ghotbzadeh. There would be continuous exchanges between the Secretary-General himself and Tehran. The conflicts and power struggle between Council member, Bani-Sadr, and Ghotbzadeh was temporarily assuaged by Waldheim's appearance in Tehran. Bani-Sadr's earlier discussions with the United Nations had been resented by the new flamboyant Foreign Minister. This latest show belonged to Ghotbzadeh. The Foreign Minister, now in the international limelight and personally impressed with Waldheim's desire for objectivity, was one more important force in Iran who was willing to begin discussions.

The "Waldheim Plan," if one could call it that, was meant to save face for both parties concerned. The hostages must be released. It was an illegal act. If the United Nations in any way appeared to recognize it differently, it could destroy that diplomatic body itself. What the United Nations could do, quite separately from the hostage question, was appoint an international commission to hear the grievances of the Iranian people. The "crimes" of the Shah and his government, the interference of America and its exploitation of the Iranian people could all be aired.

This was much too weak from the Iranian standpoint, but, rather than hardening their position, it had strangely drawn them into dialogue. Sadegh Ghotbzadeh appeared to take on the personal challenge of convincing Waldheim of the legitimacy of Iranian complaints, with spectacular success. A member of the Secretary-General's staff referred to the activities of the former Shah's SAVAK as "disgusting."

Waldheim himself, shaken by the visit, promised he would "bring this message of suffering before the United Nations, before the world community. We shall certainly do what-

The Canadian Caper

ever we can to ensure that this mutilation of human beings will never take place again."

Most significantly, the Secretary-General's visit was hailed by the Iranians as a national triumph, and, thus, a source of great confidence for them. It was an American-held hope that this self-proclaimed Tehran victory might lead to more negotiations and dialogue.

But there were no illusions in Qum. Iran quietly went about its work of transferring funds from European banks. The American-proposed U.N. economic sanctions against Iran appeared on the way.

The Secretary-General returned to New York on January 4, cutting short his seven-day mission. Officially, it was said there was urgent business at the United Nations, but Waldheim could see it was useless for him to stay further. Both the Secretary-General and the Iranian authorities announced the visit as "very helpful," the U.N. diplomat saying they had "a very extensive exchange of views with the different aspects of the problem." Ghotbzadeh added, "It was not a matter of making progress, but the fact that we exchanged views." But, successful as the event had been in Iran and allowing for the future fruits of the meeting, the immediate reaction of violence directed against the international diplomat had outraged most of the world even further.

When the hostage crisis had first begun, the Ayatollah Khomeini had assumed time would be on his side. The event had galvanized his people behind a united theme just when they were at the very brink of civil war. The diversion promised to give the government time to get its economy straightened out. And, when it came to dealing with America, Vietnam had taught that "the corrupt, indulgent U.S. giant was too impatient to hold out long."

The Carter administration had fooled the old mullah, both by its cautious shedding of its Vietnamese-syndrome, its apparent domestic unity, and by an uncharacteristically American, uncommonly superb diplomatic offensive. Khomeini had needed the Waldheim mission. Events were deteriorating. Time had turned out to be the Ayatollah's enemy after all. Assassinations were now common in Iran. At least two members of the Revolutionary Council had been killed. An anti-clerical group called Forqhan was now publicly claiming responsibility.

The Sharietmadari-Khomeini joint call for unity was coming unpatched. Tribal unrest in the outlying provinces was growing to alarming

The Canadian Caper

proportions. The Sunni Kurds were now openly fighting a religious war against the Shiite Ayatollah who had promised them freedom if they supported his revolution. The effects of the new constitution were beginning to reach Kurdistan where people had finally realized that, not only had Khomeini betrayed them, but even more insultingly, he had instituted Shiite Islam as the religion of the State. Sunni Muslims near the Pakistani border in Baluchistan rioted, killing ten. In Khuzestan, the Sunni Arabs continued their daily sabotage of the pipelines, further disrupting the already crippled oil supply.

But the worst violence was occurring in Azerbaijan province in the north. Azerbaijani rebels had been fighting for their independence since the days of old Reza Shah, then a young, fierce, Cossack lieutenant. Invoking the name of Sharietmadari, himself a Shiite but an ayatollah they felt they could trust, mobs controlled the streets of major Azerbaijani cities, and snipers took a deadly toll of Revolutionary militia by night.

Khomeini was in trouble. The domestic crisis could mean the fragmentation of his people. The Russian army, massed on his borders, began to occupy his thoughts more each day. The threat of U.N. economic sanctions could be a final blow to a tottering economy. But if the seventy-nine-year-old mullah was heartened by Waldheim's visit, he did not betray even a smile. The hostage question would remain deadlocked. First, Iran had to follow its constitutional process. A new president was to be elected. Perhaps Khomeini's new government, inaccurately heralded as the first elected in the history of the Persian people, could deal with an Iran gone crazy.

While President Jimmy Carter's political fortune continued its extraordinary recovery in January, there were some signs of danger. Some politicians questioned how long the crisis could continue without working against the incumbent. Presidential contenders now openly debated America's role in Iran.

Most serious was the beginning of an erosion of American allied support. France openly balked at stern measures that would offend Iran and her oil, and quickly refused to participate in an Olympic boycott, giving every appearance of seeking to establish her own détente with the Russians. West Germany was straddling the fence.

But, on January 29, Americans learned they still had some committed allies when the wraps came off a complex rescue mission. Banner

The Canadian Caper

headlines announced, "Canadians Help Six Americans Flee Iran."

The six American consular and agricultural officials and their wives had fled the embassy the very hour of the takeover, on November 4. Realizing their danger, they had huddled together in a tiny cottage for several days. Terrified they would be discovered by the angry Iranians, they had called Ken Taylor, the Canadian Ambassador, asking for refuge. With the tedious, unglamourous mechanics of a John le Carré hero, the handsome Canadian diplomat had secreted the six away in various homes throughout the city. Gracious hosts treated them as honored house guests. Fearing to go out, except for absolutely necessary ventures, the Americans spent so much time playing Scrabble, that, as one escapee told it, they could tell the letter of a Scrabble tile just by looking at the wood grain on the back.

The long, boring days were interrupted once when an owner decided to sell one of the houses. With the prospect of strangers parading through, it was necessary to quickly find another shelter. Like a scene from a spy movie, the diplomats were stealthily rushed away to a new hiding place.

After the Christmas visit of the three American clergymen, the controversy over the hostage question threatened to blow their cover. By January 15, it was reestablished that there were, indeed, fifty hostages held in the embassy, but the investigations and inquiry may have aroused curious neighbors or compromised their few contacts.

On January 19, the telephone rang, and an anonymous voice insisted "on speaking to Mr. and Mrs. (Joseph) Stafford," two of the hiding diplomats. The game was up.

Ken Taylor and his embassy staff held tense, hushed discussions, deciding finally to evacuate all Canadians living in the country, close their embassy and escape with the Americans. In their last few hours in Iran, with Revolutionary agents closing in on the conspiracy, the Americans were handed their CIA-prepared passports. The forged documents showed them as Canadian diplomats. With great trepidation, the caravan made the tense trip to the Tehran Airport, only rejoicing when the plane left the air space of Iran. Left behind at the Canadian embassy, a forlorn little sign hung on the doorknob, "Embassy closed for the day."

The double risks which Canada took were not wasted on Washington. Americans realized full well the sacrifice Canada made in closing her embassy in Tehran, and the great personal danger to her diplomats.

The Canadian Caper

The United States exploded with joy and gratitude. Red maple leaves bloomed on school bulletin boards, magazines reported in great detail the complicated maneuvers of North America's most celebrated "spy caper." American billboards, editorials and letters to the editor praised their friend to the north. In a full page *New York Times* advertisement, Citicorp thanked Canada, "In a world filled with hatred, anxiety and spite, you showed your unwavering compassion, reason, and courage." Congress voted 370-0 to acclaim Canada and her people, for showing the "entire world that . . . honorable commitment toward civilized ideals of international conduct cannot be shaken by terrorist threats." Congressional history had no precedent for the honor.

In Tehran, Iranian mobs passed by the former Canadian embassy and glared in, hoping to find someone or something to vent their anger upon. Foreign Minister Ghotbzadeh denounced Canada's action as an act of "espionage, and a violation of international law." The sputtering Iranian spokesman warned that Canada "will sooner or later pay for this duplicity and cheating."

In spite of foot dragging by some allies, America was cheered. She was not alone.

10

The Return of Bani-Sadr

With the specter of the giant Soviet bear hulking on the Iranian border and with the American spirit renewed by the escape of the six hostages, Iran prepared for its first presidential election ever under the new Islamic constitution. One hurdred and six candidates were running, Khomeini charging that many of them were "brainless perverts." The large field was said to be another CIA ploy designed to cause confusion. The Ayatollah took the liberty of paring the field down to a more manageable ten candidates, including the powerful Foreign Minister Ghotbzadeh, the recently discredited Economics Minister Abolhassan Bani-Sadr, Health Minister Kazem Sani and Admiral Ahmad Madani.

In a bitter confrontation, demonstrating that

politics could be as ruthless under the new constitution as the old, Jalaleddin Farsi, the highly respected candidate of the Islamic Republic Party, was disqualified. It was learned that his father was an Afghan. The new constitution allowed that only "pure Iranians" could lead the people.

With Farsi's bitterly contested elimination, the favorite appeared to be Abolhassan Bani-Sadr, foreign minister at the time of the embassy takeover and, to Western audiences, the man with the comical "Groucho Marx face." Bani-Sadr, showing more moderation and flexibility than his Imam, had been responsible for obtaining the release of the thirteen hostages and had spoken out in opposition to any trial of the Americans still at the embassy. His moderation had gotten him fired.

But things were different in Iran now. Crowds who demonstrated at the embassy lacked the fire and hatred of earlier days. Sometimes Taleghani Street was deserted. Unrest in the outer provinces was crippling the country. Lack of responsible leadership in industry had further destroyed the economy. The Russian threat was gaining much credibility as news spread of massive Soviet Army formations facing the border. Khomeini's health was a concern. If the Imam died, the nation could be

The Return of Bani-Sadr

plunged into a terrifying civil war.

Khomeini's office issued a communiqué, endorsing no candidate, but urging the populace to vote. The voting was, indeed, described as "enthusiastic" and soon an apparent trend appeared. In a field of ten candidates, Bani-Sadr was running away with the election.

The U.S. State Department was cautious but there could be no doubt that Washington was pleased. Though no friend of the United States, at least Bani-Sadr had no personal ax to grind. He was an educated man, by Revolutionary standards, a reasonable man, a man of competence.

The most surprising result of the election was the size of Bani-Sadr's victory. Outdistancing his many rivals with seventy-six percent of the vote, the Economics Minister could have claimed a landlside even in a two-man race. Foreign Minister Sadegh Ghotbzadeh, whose swaggering apery of what he perceived to be party line was virtually always negated by Khomeini and the militants, had to share votes with the bottom seven candidates.

For such a clear mandate to emerge from the confusion was a hopeful sign for the future. Iran seemed to have a national opinion. With Bani-Sadr's views so widely known, it was thought to be a vote for moderation. It was interpreted by some as a statement to the government to resolve its international conflicts and get on with the much neglected work of rebuilding the economy.

But the appearance of national unity was soon shown to be another Iranian illusion. The separatists had refused to vote. Kurdish rebels in at least two cities did not even open polls, and it appeared that Sharietmadari himself may have boycotted the election. Nevertheless, by January 27, the complex voting procedure had been completed without, as Revolutionary Council members put it, "a serious hitch." "At long last, the people had their chance to speak." For the first time in modern history, the Revolutionaries proclaimed, "Iran had legally chosen its own leader without fraud."

On January 28, President-elect Bani-Sadr set his jaw and parroted the Imam's line. Only when America "abandons its expansionist policies and respects the sovereignty of other nations" will the crisis be resolved. The rhetoric was tough, but there was no condition of returning the Shah. Washington watched and listened closely to find an opening.

On Friday, February 1, West German Ambassador to the United Nations, Rudiger von Wechmar, made a stunning announcement. A plan devised by Secretary-General Kurt

The Return of Bani-Sadr

Waldheim could obtain the release of the hostages within weeks. Under the proposal, an international commission of inquiry would be sent to Iran to listen to complaints, after which the hostages could be removed from the militants and sent to a "staging camp," hopefully in the hands of the International Red Cross. Though Washington was disappointed in the statement that this would take "weeks" instead of "days," the announcement seemed to herald good news, a breakthrough in the long, horrendous stalemate.

In Tehran, it was the Muslim Sabbath and no news of the announcement was released. Thousands of faithful Muslims gathered outside the hospital where the Ayatollah Khomeini was recuperating from a heart ailment. Arms uplifted, fervent prayers were led by mullahs in celebration of the first anniversary of Khomeini's return from exile. In other Iranian cities as well, prayerful, emotional marches through the streets honored the Imam. There was no reported violence.

On February 4, Tehran announced that the "Waldheim plan" was acceptable. The excitement was heightened by news reports that the families of the hostages were flying to Washington for briefings. Although most relatives declined to speak to reporters, their faces wore smiles brighter than had been seen in nearly 100 days of American humiliation. "There is a glimmer of hope," one man acknowledged. The State Department's almost total clampdown on news releases heightened speculation that sensitive negotiations were taking place.

That same Monday, the militants reiterated their constant, continuing demand that the Shah be returned before the hostages be released. But they also announced their invitation to a private, fifty-person group of Americans who were to arrive on Wednesday, not to discuss the hostages, but to learn about the Iranian revolution.

Meanwhile, in a hospital blocks away from Taleghani Street, Bani-Sadr stood before his ailing Imam, humbly accepting the *firman*, or decree, which officially installed him as Iran's first president. Turning to television cameras, he pledged to cleanse Iran of the hundreds of years of corruption, which he blamed on centuries of greedy, self-serving monarchies. "We are facing great difficulties," he acknowledged, "but I am sure that we will overcome them, thanks to the powerful will of our nation."

Still within the glow of his seventy-six percent mandate, Bani-Sadr wasted no time in establishing his direction. The militants in the embassy "are not the government," he said.

The Return of Bani-Sadr

"The American press might be welcomed back. False reports are better than no reports." He mentioned a possible boycott of the Olympic games in Moscow and aid to Afghan rebels, sending out a warning to the people that the ego-inflating contest with America notwithstanding, the Soviets may be their real and tangible enemy.

The first real test of presidential power came on February 6 when, in a radio broadcast, the embassy militants accused Nasser Minachi, Minister of Information and National Guidance, of having "close links with the CIA." Without governmental authorization, agents descended on Minachi, hauling him out of his bed at midnight and throwing him into prison to await further pronouncements by the students.

The action triggered outrage in Bani-Sadr, who denounced the embassy militants as "dictators" creating "a government within a government." Minachi was ordered released. The President angrily told a Tehran newspaper that the militants were "paving the way for lawlessness" in Iran. "How could you expect a government employee to go to work feeling secure," he said, "when there is no legal or judicial security in the country? That will undoubtedly lead to disorder."

The following day, the Kuwaiti newspaper, *Al Khadaf*, reported that Revolutionary guards-

THE IRAN CRISIS

men were to relieve the militants and take charge of the hostages. The terrorists were said to be banned from Iranian airwaves. Deputy Secretary of State Warren Christopher, although chary in his optimism, told American viewers on the NBC "Today" show, "We have a somewhat promising situation and we are working hard on it." The long-awaited U.S.-sponsored economic sanctions were being largely played down by the State Department. The situation held promise for resolution.

If indeed there was now a chance to end the crisis, the United States as a whole welcomed the news with muted optimism. With Bani-Sadr's return, there had been a sense of inevitability about the release of the hostages, but ironically, not a corresponding increase in interest. It was as if the American nation were tiring of the event; their frustration having been vented, the actual release of their fellow countrymen would be anticlimactic. In their television-oriented world, this was a "special" that had lasted too long. Due in no small part to Carter's handling of the crisis, the American public had held well. Now, just when some flexibility or compromise might allow the new Iranian President an excuse to release the embassy captives, the American mood was shifting.

But, if the rise of Bani-Sadr and his apparent

The Return of Bani-Sadr

willingness to negotiate was anticlimactic to most Americans, it was exhilarating news indeed for the hostages' families. Mrs. Louisa Kennedy, working daily at the State Department crisis telephones, told reporters, "I feel a great renewal of hope. I think tensions are lessening now. There's something more constructive in the air." She added reassuringly, "Some spirit is moving us in the right direction on all this, and it's not coming from this country alone. It's coming from Iran too."

At the National Cathedral in Washington, a service was conducted for the hostages' families. A letter from Chargé d'Affaires Bruce Laingen to his son was read from the pulpit. "All this, too, will pass," Laingen wrote. "I remain convinced that there is decency and respect in every human being. Never lose your sense of openness and tolerance for others." It was a message of hope, not only for a son, but also for a nation.

With tensions lessening, about thirty of the hostages were visited by Ahmad Khomeini, the Imam's son, and Hilarion Capudji, former Greek Catholic Archbishop of Jerusalem, on Friday, February 8. The meeting was televised by the students, and eventually seen in America, the first sight ever of hostage Kathryn Koob, an early hero in the critical hours of the embassy takeover. Koob laughed and cried, telling the former Archbishop that he was "the answer to a prayer."

The next day, John Thomas, an American Indian activist, was allowed to visit with a captive U.S. Marine, Paul Lewis, for ten minutes, and found him to be in "perfect" condition. "He looked too good to be a hostage," reported Lewis.

On Monday, February 11, the one-hundredth day of captivity for the hostages came and went, with no release in sight. When a group of Americans visiting Tehran by invitation of the militants were allowed to enter the embassy and talk with the students, President Bani-Sadr responded with another denunciation of the militants. "I will not accept such behavior," he told a Tehran newspaper. "In my capacity as president of this government, I call on the students to put an end to this and to unify their opinions and actions with the government's opinion."

But the general mood in Tehran that Monday was one of celebration. For America, it was the one-hundredth day of captivity, but for Iran, it was the first anniversary of the Revolutionary government, the day when the Shah's last prime minister, Shahpour Bakhtiar, resigned and the power passed to the Revolutionary Council. A giant parade of army, police and Revolutionary

The Return of Bani-Sadr

guards and committees was planned for the celebration. Thousands turned out for the event; reviewing stands were full. Ironically, several died in the crush of the celebration, while the crisis which had brought one of the most powerful nations on earth perilously close to war had still not yet involved the shedding of blood.

In the afternoon, President Bani-Sadr granted an interview to the French newspaper, *Le Monde*. The Iranian leader laid down strict guidelines for the release of the hostages. Admitting that the Imam had not yet endorsed his plan, but claiming unanimity from the Council, Bani-Sadr's conditions included the U.S. acknowledgment of "crimes" against the Iranian people, including the 1953 CIA overthrow of Mossadegh. Further, the United States must recognize the right of Iran to "obtain the extradition of the Shah and the restitution of his fortune," and to "no longer interfere in our affairs."

The State Department's immediate reaction was to announce that there would be no blanket admission of so-called crimes. However, spokesmen admitted that negotiations were in a "very sensitive stage," and all statements from Washington became more guarded or nonexistent.

Plans for the international "tribunal" or "commission" continued. Waldheim was reported to be in daily contact with both the U.S. and Iranian officials. Revolutionary Council Secretary Mohammed Beheshti indicated that a solution might be possible before the March 14 parliamentary elections. Foreign Minister Ghotbzadeh announced that the international commission might be able to begin its work in Tehran within the week. President Bani-Sadr said that perhaps the hostages could be released before the commission completed its job. He cautioned, however, that giving up the hostages would not mean Iran had given up its demand for the extradition of the Shah.

"We will be after the Shah's extradition until Resurrection Day," he pledged. "It does not mean that we will free them and then he can have a good time over there."

Bani-Sadr continued his daily attacks on the militants in the embassy, patiently maneuvering to break the political stranglehold of the students. The U.S. State Department remained quiet. "Official comment on each and every proposal is neither necessary nor productive," Hodding Carter announced.

On February 14, the new President of Iran advised that the Imam, Khomeini, had approved the three-point plan whereby the hostages could be released if the United States agreed. It was a tantalizing proposition. "There

The Return of Bani-Sadr

is a plan on President Carter's desk," Bani-Sadr said, "if he accepts, [it] can lead to the release of the hostages in forty-eight hours." In a statement reminiscent of the Shah's 1942 demand to both Russia and Great Britain, Bani-Sadr insisted on a U.S. guarantee of his country's geopolitical and economic independence. Further, the Iranian President gave a revealing glimpse of his country's economic deterioration when he added that "we depend on the United States for spare parts. They are essential for us."

Much more significant than Bani-Sadr's public announcement was his private message to the American President passed along secret channels. If, in addition to a U.N. Commission, Carter would issue a statement of regret for past U.S.-Iranian policy, the release of the hostages could take place immediately.

The response in Washington was swift. In a nationally televised press conference, Carter announced to his nation that "positive progress" had been made toward the hostages' release. He further stated that the United States was willing to accept the proposal of an international commission to settle the conflict. But there was clearly, unequivocally no statement of regret.

Iran and the United States mutually accepted Waldheim's proposal for an international inquiry, but they remained divided on what and how the United States should define its past policy. The waiting began. On February 15, Ghotbzadeh announced that "the tribunal," as he insisted it should be called, could be formed "within a few hours," but he reiterated demands that the hostages could not be released until "the tribunal" finished its work.

Former Irish Foreign Minister and U.N. official Sean MacBride disagreed. "The commission could hardly begin its work until the hostages have been released," he said. "Either they are released before the commission meets or they could be released concurrently with the setting up of the commission."

Other reports suggested that, in a compromise move, the hostages could be transferred to a third country, perhaps Algeria, and placed in the hands of the Red Cross pending completion of the tribunal.

Ghotbzadeh told reporters that Secretary-General Waldheim had called him at 3:00 A.M. to discuss the members of the panel. In an hourlong phone conversation, the members were agreed upon. We are "waiting only for their acceptance," Ghotbzadeh said. "For us, the names aren't important. What is important is that the commission is formed."

By Saturday, February 16, what the Iranians

The Return of Bani-Sadr

were calling a tribunal, and what the United Nations was calling a commission had still not been officially announced. That evening U.N. sources began to slowly leak the news. The commission members would include Edmond Louis Pettiti of France, head of the Paris Bar Association; Adib Daoudy, a foreign affairs specialist from Syria; Andres Aguilar, a diplomat from Venezuela; Mohamed Bedjaoui, Ambassador to the United Nations from Algeria; and Abu Sayeed Chowdhurry, former President of Bangladesh. U.N. spokesmen stated that the five were expected to arrive in New York on Monday for a meeting with Secretary-General Waldheim, and would leave for Tehran by the end of the week.

On Sunday, February 17, hopes for early release of the hostages suddenly faded again. Bani-Sadr, in a more obdurate statement than at any time since his election, announced that the hostages might be released only after the commission completed its job and the United States "undertakes its obligations" to Iran.

The Iranian President pointed to "the unsolved return of the Shah from Panama," but sources in Iran and Washington concluded that Bani-Sadr was miffed that Carter had "missed" a chance to solve the stalemate with a "simple statement of regret."

THE IRAN CRISIS

In Washington, State Department spokesmen refused to comment on the new, more rigid comments of the Iranian President. "We are staying with the policy of not commenting on the situation in Iran until further notice," said press officer David Nall.

That week, the new hard line was reiterated by an increasingly tough Bani-Sadr, who announced that Khomeini was in "complete agreement" with his plan not to release the hostages until the United States "undertakes its obligations." The international tribunal inquiry would not be sufficient.

There was weariness at the United Nations. Some rationalized that the Iranian and American presidents were only acting out previously agreed upon movements to assure domestic support for their eventual compromise decision. Others more realistically feared that Khomeini's extraordinary and irrational influence had once more seeped into the situation and the tedious process may need major repairs.

American Secretary of State Cyrus Vance flew to New York for talks with Secretary-General Waldheim. Although the trip was officially dismissed as "general discussion," a spokeswoman admitted that "the subject of Iran will probably come up."

Meanwhile, in the American embassy in

The Return of Bani-Sadr

Tehran, there was evidently growing despair. A letter received from Marine Sergeant Kevin Hermening, addressed to his parents, warned that he was planning an escape. The youngest American captive revealed great mental depression and personal contempt toward his jailers. Preparing his family for a possible violent conclusion to events, Hermening told them he would rather die trying to get out than remain a hostage any longer. The crisis, which appeared to be on its way into a fifth month, was just as dangerous and tense as it had been on November 4. The same elements remained. The careful steps that had been laid toward a solution were indeed fragile. The work of reconciliation and peace was an elusive business.

11

The U.N. Commission

At the end of February, 1980, with snow falling outside their windows, Iranian officials began to agonize over the impending visit of the U.N. Commission. It was viewed by most in the Revolutionary Council as a breakthrough, a chance to tell their story to the world. But typically, there was great division among them.

Accepting the U.N. panel would give an almost irreversible momentum to the release of the hostages, a decision that some Islamic clergymen openly opposed. The civilian government of Abolhassan Bani-Sadr with its overwhelming mandate was slipping beyond the reach of the clerical grasp. To strengthen the government's hand even further, the ailing Ayatollah Khomeini unexpectedly announced that Bani-Sadr would henceforth be Commander-in-Chief of the Armed Forces.

Well aware of the volatility of Iranian politics, the Tehran government urged Waldheim to hold off a few days. Things were under control but Bani-Sadr wanted to consolidate his strength. The opposition was testy. Iran must be prepared for the coming of the commission. Foreign Minister Sadegh Ghotbzadeh rushed home from a European tour to help prepare the groundwork.

But, on Wednesday, February 27, a cloud once again descended on the prospect of a solution. Either out of fear that the initiative would be lost, or as his detractors have it, in order to spotlight the U.N.'s role in the negotiations, Secretary General Kurt Waldheim dispatched his commission to Geneva. That hasty, seemingly innocent, decision posed special problems for the government in Iran.

If the Bani-Sadr government waved the Commission on to Tehran, it would arouse the fury of the militants and Islamic clergy who were still debating the validity of Waldheim's plan. The only other choice, postponing the visit altogether, would deny the Iranians the very victory they had won. By leaving the distinguished U.N. panel stranded on the tarmac at the Geneva Airport, it would look to the

The U.N. Commission

world as if Iran were trying to avoid an American-Waldheim imposed solution. Lost in all of this confusion was the fact that the Bani-Sadr government had superbly negotiated one of its few victories in the entire crisis, namely that of turning around U.S. policy to allow a hearing of Iranian grievances even before the release of hostages. The domestic use of that powerful victory would be lost if Iran now appeared to be a reluctant party to events. U.N. Commission member Mohammed Bedjaoui of Algeria and his colleagues faced newsmen for a few hours in Geneva and then were suddenly called back to New York. The trip was off.

When the smoke finally cleared and the Commission was indeed brought into Tehran, President Bani-Sadr announced that the U.N.'s work was "unrelated" to the hostage question. This new hard line, designed to neutralize his Islamic militant opposition and make up for the Geneva fiasco, was devastating news to the American public. Privately forewarned and assured by Tehran that events were, in spite of appearances, still on course, the U.S. State Department remained more optimistic. But the Bani-Sadr statement, regardless of the logical intent behind it, backfired.

The Ayatollah Khomeini, convalescing in a

THE IRAN CRISIS

Tehran residence and having for some time appeared quite indifferent to events, suddenly aroused like a lion awakening from its sleep. What now looked in Iran as Bani-Sadr's new tough stubborn stand before merciless American pressure, evidently came too close to Khomeini territory. It was the Ayatollah, not his young disciple-President, who was the tamer of superpowers. The hostages could not be released anyway, Khomeini matter-of-factly announced. It was a decision for the new Iranian Majlis or parliament to make. The parliamentary elections would take place March 16. The Majlis would convene April 7.

Thus, the expected release of the hostages was once more frustrated. Triggered by a premature move by the U.N. Secretary General, events had fallen into place like a chain reaction of tumbling dominoes, with the participants themselves watching helplessly. Bani-Sadr, emasculated by Khomeini's decision, withdrew from the stage while his now allied Foreign Minister took up the attack to get the hostages released.

By March, the confusing political struggle in Iran was at last forming a picture to the outside world. The Islamic Republic Party, whose leading candidate in the presidential election had been disqualified, was still shrewdly repre-

The U.N. Commission

sented by Mohammed Beheshti and others on the Revolutionary Council. Having found himself under Council discipline in January and having seen his party lose its chance to gain the presidency, Beheshti now maneuvered for a parliamentary majority.

The hostages were becoming the tool of Bani-Sadr's opposition. As the new president moved toward resolution, Beheshti and the clergy could arouse the people against "appeasement." But as long as the hostage crisis remained unresolved, the government was paralyzed from moving against the incredible economic problems.

Torn between sympathy for his clerical colleagues and his determination not to undermine his own elected president and former student, the Ayatollah Khomeini's position was, as always, the linchpin. The State Department had concluded that the old man was neither as sinister as they had once held or as righteous as his followers insisted. The fact was that the old mullah was impressionable. His erratic moves could change as suddenly as the wind but they depended more on who was whispering in his ear than on some inspired intuition or calculated decision. When Khomeini began admonishing the people to vote against America in the upcoming election, an apparent call to support the Islamic clergy and keep the hostages, it became finally evident to Washington that its carefully negotiated agreements with Waldheim and Bani-Sadr could be tumbled by a frail breath from the old Ayatollah. Bani-Sadr's 76-percent presidential election mandate had simply evaporated.

Though the report to the U.N. Commission was largely overshadowed by Iranian political events, President Bani-Sadr had successfully galvanized his government agencies to put on their best show. On the first day, Ali Reza Nobari of the Central Bank documented the Shah's systematic exploitation of the national economy. Fifty-six billion dollars were allegedly diverted into the coffers of the Pahlavi family. But the real story, the harrowing tale of SAVAK, the Shah's Secret Police, began unfolding that Wednesday. The Bani-Sadr government provided a documented account of the innocent evolution of SAVAK—how it eventually became what was described as the "monstrous tool" of the Shah.

The tale, according to the Bani-Sadr government, began in 1949. Shortly after the attempt on his life, Mohammed Reza Pahlavi was said to have grimly set about gaining absolute control of the country. The plan of assassination

The U.N. Commission

had been hatched by a coalition of the Communist Tudeh and right-wing religious groups. The Shah, allegedly motivated by revenge, sought an ally, someone he could trust, to ferret out all of Mossadegh's supporters and the leading elements of the secretive Tudeh. He found his man in Teymur Bakhtiar, (no relation to Pahlavi's last prime minister), a general who had helped and supported the monarchy during the 1953 coup.

Bakhtiar was described to the U.N. Commission as a man without pity, celebrated for his cruelty and bravery. The Shah had first rewarded his faithfulness by appointing him military governor of Tehran. Bakhtiar was accused of taking this assignment with zest and passion, emptying the Old Reza Shah's infamous prison at Ghars and filling it with almost three thousand of the opposition. There were allegations of beatings and torture.

In 1956, SAVAK was established with Bakhtiar at the head. Agents of the new secret police were sent to McLean, Virginia, for training under the American CIA, and later, according to the Bani-Sadr government, to the Israeli MOSAD for "graduate school."

For a time, Bakhtiar was said to have used the SAVAK for his own political ends, garnering dossiers on virtually everyone, and, in the process, building one of the world's most obscene personal financial empires. Only eight years after his appointment as military governor, it was said he could look down on Tehran from a million-dollar marble palace in the upper city. Scattered around the country were nineteen other estates, including an exotic palace on the Caspian Sea and eleven productive plantations, crowned with sumptuous villas. When he tired of life in Iran, Bakhtiar could slip away to one of his three European homes, drawing freely on inexhaustible secret foreign bank accounts.

Teymur was said to have carefully cultivated the image of a man who enjoyed the shadier side of his work. While the Shah's government explained this away as legend or even necessary imagery to inspire fear, there is evidence that he experienced emotional and sadistic pleasure in his primitive methods. A persistent prison story had Bakhtiar sitting back with a grin on his face, while a helpless prisoner was forced to watch a chained and muzzled bear attack his own wife. (U.N. Commissioners were told that this incredible event was staged more than once with more than one prisoner and wife involved.)

But alas, Bakhtiar's insatiable thirst could not be quenched. Neither his mercy, nor his power, nor the perverse pleasure he allegedly

The U.N. Commission

took from dominating his helpless prisoners could satisfy his ambitions. With an immense file on Tehran's citizens, he began to plan a coup d'état against the King himself. Reports of Bakhtiar's treachery began to filter back to the palace. In a fearsome showdown, Shah Mohammed Reza confronted the nation's secret police chief and ordered him into exile. It was potentially a dangerous mistake. Not accustomed to defeat, Bakhtiar was said to have plotted and planned, fomenting riots in Tehran and unrest within the ranks; assasination attempts were common. But Teymur Bakhtiar, like many before him and many who followed, underestimated his monarch.

In August, 1970, two Iranians, claiming to be friends of the former SAVAK head, captured a plane and flew to Baghdad. Days later, the terrible Teymur Bakhtiar was dead, supposedly the victim of a hunting accident. In later years, when a bold reporter insisted the Shah must surely know who murdered the SAVAK head, the King had merely smiled and said, "We did."

Nematollah Nassiri, fat, dissolute, his face pock-marked, became the Shah's newly appointed master of SAVAK. Described to the U.N. panel as a character out of the motion picture, *Z*, Nassiri was said to have been kept on a palace leash. Never again would the Shah let his national police stray too far from the throne. The all-important dossiers would be held by Mohammed Pahlavi.

Under Nassiri, SAVAK became a fanatical political instrument for the Shah. Every political official was tailed by a SAVAK operative. Every move was examined for traitorous activity. At the university, there was said to be one SAVAK agent for every three students. Journalists were visited regularly and told what they could and could not report.

At the time of the Shah's magnificent golden coronation, where thousands hailed him as a beneficent ruler, General Nassiri was accused of expelling over twenty-five thousand people from Tehran. They were regarded as "undesirable." During the glittering twenty-five-hundredth anniversary, people arriving in Persepolis were searched by three concentric circles of guards, with the SAVAK arresting several thousand of the "troublesome element," to ensure a peaceful and elegant world celebration.

The Bani-Sadr government produced documents with the Shah himself defending the actions of his secret police, claiming that he was trying to bring his nation from the seventh to the twentieth century in twenty-five years,

The U.N. Commission

and, to do so, a country "has to be driven, and, while it sets to work, defended against those who would hinder the process. To leave saboteurs to operate in freedom would certainly not have permitted realization of this program."

For three days, 1,700 victims of the Shah's secret police paraded before the U.N. Commission. One typical young man, claiming to be apolitical but accused of being a Communist, told of arriving at the Shah's court only to be confronted with his own confession. The accused had explained to the court that the statement was phony and he had been forced to sign. This typical testimony, amazingly enough still on record, told a tale of arrest and torture. Taken to a cellar, he was allegedly stripped and beaten. Bruised and bleeding, the student says he was shoved through a door into a small, dark, unventilated toilet where he remained for a week, cowering on the damp floor, his cold, naked body wrapped only in a coarse blanket. He ate small pieces of bread thrown into his cell once a day.

Nassar Sadegh was ready to recount his story of a pistol-whipping, causing internal bleeding. Sadegh's tale, first told to the French *Le Monde* in 1972, described how two of his friends were dragged to a white-hot metal table, thrust onto it, and strapped down, their backs and chests seared like hamburger on a grill.

Riza Rizai, who had escaped the SAVAK's clutches, told of a cellmate who was buckled into a type of electric chair. After four hours of screaming agony, the burns reached his spinal column. The smell of acrid flesh remained for days, causing prisoners and jailers alike to shun the little cubicle where Riza lay with his burned cellmate, stinking like a piece of garbage. Incredibly, the man was alive to confirm Riza's tale, but after three operations, he would have to crawl into the U.N. Commissioner's hearing to tell his story.

Aside from the Revolutionary government's own prepared case, Bani-Sadr drew on evidence accumulated by Amnesty International. The Nobel Prize-winning human rights organization reported that "alleged methods of torture include whipping and beating, electric shocks, the extraction of nails and teeth, boiling water pumped into the rectum, heavy weights hung on the testicles, tying the prisoner to a white-hot table, insertion of a broken bottle into the anus and rape." In the reports issued even before the fall of the Shah, Amnesty International accused SAVAK of arresting people for simply reading banned books or for keeping treasured photographs of Khomeini or Prime Minister Mossadegh.

The U.N. Commission

Ali Akbar Hashemi Rafsanjani, a member of the Revolutionary Council, testified that SAVAK held him down, flaying the soles of his feet with an electric cable until the "bones jutted out." Other witnesses presented pictures of alleged victims, women who were tortured to death, with their breasts savagely mutilated. The U.N. panel was shown torture rooms captured intact by revolutionaries, containing "all sizes of whips" and various instruments used to yank out fingernails.

SAVAK agents were reported to have been everywhere. The Shah's claim of a small force of three thousand was ridiculed. The Revolutionary government estimated as many as twenty thousand, some recruited by intimidation and blackmail. The children of some poor Iranian workers were allegedly given permission and money to enroll in American or European schools. But first they were required to become agents and, when overseas, they were told to inform on their countrymen.

But ironically, there was no SAVAK story that threatened to embarrass America more than the alleged "Zahedi parties" in Washington, D.C. With its Watergate mentality, America seemed more scandalized by the possible indiscretion of one of its own congressmen than stories of faraway people having their arms lopped off.

THE IRAN CRISIS

While serving as the Shah's Ambassador to the United States, Ardeshir Zahedi opened his Washington, D.C., residence to entertain U.S. officials, including distinguished members of the House of Representatives. One embassy staffer described an October, 1977, party as something out of *The Arabian Nights*—caviar in crystal bowls, the world's finest wines and liquers. Men sat on sumptuous pillows around the room, and, after a time, opium water pipes and hashish were hauled out and passed around. According to eyewitnesses, Zahedi commanded one of the women to dance, which began as an exotic striptease and ended in an orgy, with dozens of prostitutes pulling guests into the revelry. One House Ethics Committee staffer was quoted as saying, "If you think Koreagate's bad, just hope they never start poking around in Tehran."

But except for some nervous public officials in Washington, D.C., including at least three very famous Democratic congressmen, Zahedi's parties, like the story of SAVAK, prompted little worldwide interest. The U.N. Commissioners passed gingerly and sympathetically through evidence of the Shah's crimes and onto the subject which absorbed most people, the hostages.

The U.N. Commission

The idea of the U.N. Commission, carefully conceived by the U.S. State Department, the Iranian government, and the Secretary General's staff, had, from the beginning, been touted as "the solution." The world would hear Iranian grievances, the hostages would be removed to the custody of the Revolutionary government of Iran and eventually freed. Though not formally signed, it was openly referred to by both sides as a "gentleman's agreement." With the chance of freedom for the Americans temporarily postponed, the U.N. panel was now directed to visit with the hostages and interview them free from the intimidating presence of their student militant jailers.

It was not a controversial concession for the Iranian people, but throughout the first week of March, the embassy militants delayed arrangements. It was at first presumed to be a logistical problem or a misunderstanding between Bani-Sadr and the militants, who may have sensed a betrayal in the works.

With each day, the already meager interest in the Iranian grievances eroded dramatically. The issue was the hostages. They had never been completely accounted for. What was the delay? Had some of them been tortured?

By Friday, the whole U.N. Commission inquiry became a charade. It did not make much

THE IRAN CRISIS

sense to continue an inquiry into injustice and illegalities of the previous regime with the present one officially endorsing the kidnapping of diplomats and now with the growing suspicion that some were unpresentable.

Foreign Minister Sadegh Ghotbzadeh began an intense effort to get the militants to open the doors to the captured U.S. embassy. Counting on the unpredictability and physical weakness of the hospitalized Ayatollah Khomeini, the militants reiterated their vow only to obey the Imam. Confused and cautious, Khomeini had nothing to say.

By the next week, the pressure was intense. Suddenly and unexpectedly the militants announced from the embassy that "the Revolutionary Council should take the hostages, or the American spies, from us and do with them what they think best." The stunning announcement brought on a cautious celebration among some members of the Iranian government. On March 14, President Abolhassan Bani-Sadr visited the Ayatollah and left with his apparent blessing. Once again, the exhausting marathon crisis was within reach of resolution.

But, as in every other tedious moment of the Iran crisis, the wind just as suddenly reversed. And, as in every other tedious moment, it was the frail seventy-nine-year-old Islamic religious

The U.N. Commission

leader who was directing the wind. Seeking to distance himself from the government's imminent and controversial resolution of the hostage crisis and seeking to reaffirm his god-like detachment from events in general, the Ayatollah Khomeini announced that he had not taken a stand on the question of turning the captured Americans over to the Council. Calling Sadegh Ghotbzadeh a "liar," the militants in the U.S. embassy once more locked their doors.

Standing out on the runway at the Tehran Airport, the Foreign Minister made a last-ditch effort to delay the departing U.N. Commission. There was still a chance that the students would allow a visit with the hostages, Ghotbzadeh insisted. A hooded militant representative nearby made a statement and the Foreign Minister whirled on him, shaking his finger in the youth's face. They stood arguing for a while, while a U.N. Commissioner stood by in embarrassment. It was all over. The Iranian government initiative to release the hostages was dead.

And so spring came to Iran, the mountain snows began to melt, the parliament was chosen, and the people obeyed their mystic mullah, electing a powerful coalition of Islamic clergy pledging to exchange the embassy captives only for the Shah. It was the New Year on the Islamic calendar, March 18, 1980, and the seventy-nine-year-old Ayatollah Khomeini announced the release of all political prisoners except "murderers, torturers and the American hostages."

Events appeared to be in the hands of two stubborn old men, antagonists, rivals. One was the exiled King, skinny, frail, his once handsome head bobbing feebly up and down, his eyeballs bulging. He was dying of cancer, and, doctors insisted, he was almost too weak to undergo another operation. As the doors appeared to be closing in Panama, Egyptian President Anwar Sadat openly received the Shah. He was once again on Islamic soil.

The King had envisioned for his people the *Great Civilization* and, indeed, he had almost pulled it off. But His Majesty's glorious reforms had not penetrated the dark, damp, putrid cells of his own prisons, where helpless men had lain dying, cut off from the modern world, subject to the whim of their jailers whose traditions had changed little since the Middle Ages.

The other old man had somehow walked out of one of those dark prisons, bringing with him a thousand stinking ghosts, with voices the King had repressed or perhaps not even heard. Shuffling across his hospital room in Tehran

The U.N. Commission

that March, the old, sleepy-eyed Ayatollah Khomeini mumbled to a frustrated government emissary, "You're in too big of a hurry, sir. Just wait."

Appendix A

Code of Conduct for the Imperial Family

In order to maintain the high status of the Imperial family, which is respected by all Iranians, the following principles are instituted as the Code of Conduct of the Imperial family:

1. Refraining from conduct considered distasteful by social custom.
2. Refraining from any acts or actions not in keeping with the high status of the Imperial family.
3. Refraining from direct contact with public officials for the purpose of handling personal business. These matters will be handled through the Ministry of Court or His Imperial Majesty's Special Office.
4. Refraining from contacts with foreign companies or organizations which are parties

to contracts and deals with Iranian public organizations.

5. Refraining from receiving commissions for any reason whatsoever, from companies and organizations, foreign or Iranian, which are parties to contracts or deals with the Iranian government.

6. Refraining from receiving valuable gifts from persons, companies, or organizations.

7. Refraining from deals of any kind with public organizations, be it the government, organizations associated with the government, municipalities, or public organizations.

8. Refraining from direct or indirect (through third person or persons) partnership or holding shares in companies or organizations that are parties to deals with the government or public organizations.

9. Refraining from founding or holding shares in organizations or companies whose activities are not compatible with the high status of the members of the Imperial family, such as restaurants, cabarets, casinos, and the like.

10. Refraining from the use of facilities and properties belonging to government and public organizations for private use.

11. Refraining from the use—for private or commercial purposes—of the services of the employees of the government and associated

Appendix A

organizations who also have responsibilities and duties in foundations associated with the Imperial family, or related organizations.

12. Refraining from asking for special favors or making recommendations to public officials in the interest of members of the Imperial family or others.

13. Refraining from the use of legal exemptions for persons outside of the Imperial family.

14. Refraining from the use of nationalized land belonging to the government or public organizations for the purpose of profiting, for example, through construction projects or establishing commercial, service, or industrial organizations.

15. Refraining from receiving anything from persons (natural or legal) in lieu of influencing public officials in order to legalize acts which would not otherwise be eligible for profit-making (such as partnership in ownership of large pieces of land in return for registering such lands for the purpose of making profit).

16. Refraining from the use of nationalized lands for agriculture and dairy projects.

17. Refraining from accepting positions on the boards of insurance, banking, and other companies.

18. Voluntary compliance with security reg-

THE IRAN CRISIS

ulations and whatever relates to public order.

19. Protecting the prestige and respect of national values and beliefs outside of the country.

20. Refraining from contacts with foreign embassies in Iran unless through the Ministry of Court.

Appendix B

The Shah's Farewell Address

Dear People of Iran:

In the open political atmosphere, gradually developed these two recent years, you, the Iranian nation, have risen against cruelty and corruption. This revolution cannot but be supported by me, the Padeshah of Iran.

However, insecurity has reached a stage where the independence of the country is at stake. Daily life is endangered and what is most critical, the lifeline of the country, the flow of oil, has been interrupted.

I tried to form a coalition government, but this has not been possible. Therefore, a temporary government has been formed to restore order and pave the way for a national government to carry out free elections very soon.

I am aware of the alliance that has existed

between political and economic corruption. I renew my oath to be protector of the constitution and undertake that past mistakes not be repeated and [be] compensated. I hereby give assurance that government will do away with repression and corruption and that social justice will be restored, after the sacrifices you have made. . . .

At the present juncture, the Imperial Army will fill its duties in accordance with its oaths. Calm has to be restored with your cooperation.

I invite the religious leaders to help restore calm to the only Shiite country in the world.

I want political leaders to help save our Fatherland. The same goes for workers and peasants.

Let us think of Iran on the road against imperialism, cruelty, and corruption, where I shall accompany you.

Appendix C

The State of the Union Address

Mr. President, Mr. Speaker, Members of the 96th Congress, fellow citizens.

These last few months have not been an easy time for any of us. As we meet tonight, it has never been more clear that the state of our union depends on the state of the world. And tonight, as throughout our own generation, freedom and peace in the world depend on the state of our union.

The 1980s have been born in turmoil, strife, and change. This is a time of challenge to our interests and our values, and it is a time that tests our wisdom and our skills.

At this time in Iran 50 Americans are still held captive, innocent victims of terrorism and anarchy.

Also at this moment massive Soviet troops

are attempting to subjugate the fiercely independent and deeply religious people of Afghanistan.

These two acts—one of international terrorism and one of military aggression—present a serious challenge to the United States of America and indeed to all the nations of the world. Together, we will meet these threats to peace.

I am determined that the United States will remain the strongest of all nations, but our power will never be used to initiate a threat to the security of any nation or to the rights of any human being. We seek to be and to remain secure—a nation at peace in a stable world—but to be secure we must face the world as it is.

Three basic developments have helped to shape our challenges:
- the steady growth and increased projection of Soviet military power beyond its own borders;
- the overwhelming dependence of the Western democracies on oil supplies from the Middle East;
- the press of social and religious and economic and political change in many nations of the developing world—exemplified by the revolution in Iran.

Each of these factors is important in its own right. Each interacts with the others. All must

Appendix C

be faced together—squarely and courageously.

We will face these challenges and we will meet them with the best that is in us. And we will not fail.

In response to the abhorrent act in Iran, our nation has never been aroused and unified so greatly in peacetime. Our position is clear. The United States will not yield to blackmail.

We continue to pursue these specific goals:
- first, to protect the present and long-range interest of the United States;
- secondly, to preserve the lives of the Amercan hostages and to secure as quickly as possible their safe release;
- if possible, to avoid bloodshed, which might further endanger the lives of our fellow citizens;
- to enlist the help of other nations in condemning this act of violence which is shocking and violates the moral and the legal standards of a civilized world; and also,
- to convince and to persuade the Iranian leaders that the real danger to their nation lies in the north in the Soviet Union and from the Soviet troops now in Afghanistan, and that the unwarranted Iranian quarrel with the United States hampers their response to this far greater danger to them.

THE IRAN CRISIS

If the American hostages are harmed, a severe price will be paid.

We will never rest until every one of the American hostages is released.

But now we face a broader and more fundamental challenge in this region because of the recent military action of the Soviet Union.

Now, as during the last three and one-half decades, the relationship between our country, the United States of America, and the Soviet Union is the most critical factor in determining whether the world will live in peace or be engulfed in global conflict.

Since the end of the Second World War, America has led other nations in meeting the challenge of mounting Soviet power. This has not been a simple or a static relationship. Between us there has been cooperation—there has been competition—and at times there has been confrontation.

In the 1940s, we took the lead in creating the Atlantic Alliance in response to the Soviet Union's suppression and then consolidation of its East European empire and the resulting threat of the Warsaw Pact to Western Europe.

In the 1950s, we helped to contain further Soviet challenges in Korea and in the Middle East, and we re-armed, to assure the continuation of that containment.

Appendix C

In the 1960s, we met the Soviet challenges in Berlin and we faced the Cuban missile crises, and we sought to engage the Soviet Union in the important task of moving beyond the cold war and away from confrontation.

And in the 1970s, three American Presidents negotiated with the Soviet leaders in attempts to halt the growth of the nuclear arms race. We sought to establish rules of behavior that would reduce the risks of conflict, and we searched for areas of cooperation that could make our relations reciprocal and productive—not only for the sake of our two nations, but for the security and peace of the entire world

In all these actions, we have maintained two commitments: To be ready to meet any challenge by Soviet military power, and to develop ways to resolve disputes and keep the peace.

Preventing nuclear war is the foremost responsibility of the two superpowers. That is why we have negotiated the strategic arms limitation talks, treaties—SALT I and SALT II. Especially now in a time of great tension, observing the mutual constraints imposed by the terms of these treaties will be in the best interest of both countries—and will help to preserve world peace. I will consult very closely with the Congress on this matter as we strive to control nuclear weapons. That effort to control nuclear

THE IRAN CRISIS

weapons will not be abandoned.

We superpowers also have the responsibility to exercise restraint in the use of our great military force. The integrity and the independence of weaker nations must not be threatened. They must know that in our presence they are secure.

But now the Soviet Union has taken a radical and an aggressive new step. It is using its great military power against a relatively defenseless nation. The implications of the Soviet invasion of Afghanistan could pose a most serious threat to the peace since the Second World War.

The vast majority of nations on earth have condemned this latest Soviet attempt to extend its colonial domination of others and have demanded the immediate withdrawal of Soviet troops. The Moslem world is especially and justifiably outraged by this aggression against an Islamic people. No action of a world power has ever been so quickly and so overwhelmingly condemned.

But verbal condemnation is not enough. The Soviet Union must pay a concrete price for its aggression. While this invasion continues, we and the other nations of the world cannot conduct business as usual with the Soviet Union. That is why the United States has imposed stiff economic penalties on the Soviet Union. I will not issue any permits for Soviet ships to fish in

Appendix C

the coastal waters of the United States. I have cut Soviet access to high-technology equipment and agricultural products. I have limited other commerce with the Soviet Union and I have asked our allies and friends to join with us in restraining their own trade with the Soviets and not to replace our own embargoed items. And I have notified the Olympic Committee that with Soviet invading forces in Afghanistan, neither the American people nor I will support sending an Olympic team to Moscow.

The Soviet Union is going to have to answer some basic questions: Will it help promote a more stable international environment in which its own legitimate, peaceful concerns can be pursued? Or will it continue to expand its military power far beyond its genuine security needs and use that power for colonial conquest?

The Soviet Union must realize that its decision to use military force in Afghanistan will be costly to every political and economic relationship it values.

The region which is now threatened by Soviet troops in Afghanistan is of great strategic importance. It contains more than two-thirds of the world's exportable oil. The Soviet effort to dominate Afghanistan has brought Soviet military forces to within 300 miles of the Indian Ocean and close to the Straits of Hormuz—a waterway through which much of the world's oil must flow. The Soviet Union is now attempting to consolidate a strategic position, therefore, that poses a grave threat to the free movement of Middle East oil.

This situation demands careful thought, steady nerves, and resolute action—not only for this year but for many years to come. It demands collective efforts to meet this new threat to security in the Persian Gulf and in Southwest Asia. It demands the participation of all those who rely on oil from the Middle East and who are concerned with global peace and stability. And it demands consultation and close cooperation with countries in the area which might be threatened.

Meeting this challenge will take national will, diplomatic and political wisdom, economic sacrifice and, of course, military capability. We must call on the best that is in us to preserve the security of this crucial region.

Let our position be absolutely clear: An attempt by any outside force to gain control of the Persian Gulf region will be regarded as an assault on the vital interests of the United States of America and such an assault will be repelled by any means necessary, including military force.

During the past three years you have joined

Appendix C

with me to improve our own security and the prospects for peace—not only in the vital oil-producing area of the Persian Gulf region, but around the world.

We have increased annually our real commitment for defense, and we will sustain this increased effort throughout our Five-Year Defense Program. It is imperative that Congress approve this strong defense budget for 1981 encompassing a five-percent real growth in authorizations without any reductions.

We are also improving our capability to deploy U.S. military forces rapidly to distant areas.

We have helped to strengthen NATO and our other alliances, and recently we and other NATO members have decided to develop and to deploy modernized intermediate-range nuclear forces to meet an unwarranted and increased threat from the nuclear weapons of the Soviet Union.

We are working with our allies to prevent conflict in the Middle East. The peace treaty between Egypt and Israel is a notable achievement which represents a strategic asset for America and which also enhances prospects for regional and world peace. We are now engaged in further negotiations to provide full autonomy for the people of the West Bank and

Gaza, to resolve the Palestinian issue in all its aspects, and to preserve the peace and security of Israel.

Let no one doubt our commitment to the security of Israel. In a few days we will observe an historic event when Israel makes another major withdrawal from the Sinai and when ambassadors will be exchanged between Israel and Egypt.

We have also expanded our own sphere of friendship. Our deep commitment to human rights and to meeting human needs has improved our relationship with much of the Third World. Our decision to normalize relations with the People's Republic of China will help to preserve peace and stability in Asia and in the Western Pacific.

We have increased and strengthened our naval presence in the Indian Ocean, and we are now making arrangements for key naval and air facilities to be used by our forces in the region of Northeast Africa and the Persian Gulf.

We have reconfirmed our 1959 agreement to help Pakistan preserve its independence and its integrity. The United States will take action—consistent with our own laws—to assist Pakistan in resisting any outside aggression. And I am asking the Congress specifically to reaffirm this agreement. I am also working, along with

Appendix C

the leaders of other nations, to provide additional military and economic aid for Pakistan. That request will come to you in just a few days.

In the weeks ahead, we will further strengthen political and military ties with other nations in the region.

We believe that there are no irreconcilable differences between us and any Islamic nation. We respect the faith of Islam, and we are ready to cooperate with all Moslem countries.

Finally, we are prepared to work with other countries in the region to share a cooperative security framework that respects differing values and political beliefs, yet which enhances the independence, security and prosperity of all.

All these efforts combined emphasize our dedication to defend and preserve the vital interests of the region and of the Nation which we represent and those of our allies in Europe and the Pacific and also in the parts of the world which have such great strategic importance to us, stretching especially to the Middle East and Southwest Asia.

With your help I will pursue these efforts with vigor and with determination. You and I will act as necessary to protect and to preserve our Nation's security.

The men and women of America's armed forces are on duty tonight in many parts of the world. I am proud of the job they are doing and I know you share that pride. I believe that our volunteer forces are adequate for current defense needs and I hope that it will not become necessary to impose a draft. However, we must be prepared for that possibility. For this reason, I have determined that the Selective Service system must now be revitalized. I will send legislation and budget proposals to the Congress next month so that we can begin registration and then meet future mobilization needs rapidly if they arise.

We also need clear and quick passage of a new charter to define the legal authority and accountability of our intelligence agencies. We will guarantee that abuses do not recur, but we must tighten our controls on sensitive intelligence information and we need to remove unwarranted restraints on America's ability to collect intelligence.

The decade ahead will be a time of rapid change, as nations everywhere seek to deal with new problems and age-old tensions. But America need have no fear—we can thrive in a world of change if we remain true to our values and actively engage in promoting world peace.

We will continue to work as we have for peace in the Middle East and southern Africa. We will continue to build our ties with develop-

Appendix C

ing nations, respecting and helping to strengthen their national independence which they have struggled so hard to achieve, and we will continue to support the growth of democracy and the protection of human rights.

In repressive regimes, popular frustrations often have no outlet except through violence. But when peoples and their governments can approach their problems together—through open, democratic methods—the basis for stability and peace is far more solid and far more enduring.

That is why our support for human rights in other countries is in our own national interest as well as part of our own national character.

Peace—a peace that preserves freedom—remains America's first goal. In the coming years as a mighty nation, we will continue to pursue peace.

But to be strong abroad we must be strong at home. And in order to be strong, we must continue to face up to the difficult issues that confront us as a nation today.

The crises in Iran and Afghanistan have dramatized a very important lesson. Our excessive dependence on foreign oil is a clear and present danger to our nation's security.

The need has never been more urgent. At long last, we must have a clear, comprehensive energy policy for the United States.

As you well know, I have been working with the Congress in a concentrated and persistent way over the past three years to meet this need.

We have made progress together. But Congress must act promptly now to complete final action on this vital energy legislation.

Our Nation will then have a major conservation effort, important initiatives to develop solar power, realistic pricing based on the true value of oil, strong incentives for the production of coal and other fossil fuels in the United States, and our Nation's most massive peacetime investment in the development of synthetic fuels.

The American people are making progress in energy conservation. Last year we reduced overall petroleum consumption by eight percent and gasoline consumption by five percent below what it was the year before.

Now we must do more. After consultation with the Governors, we will set gasoline conservation goals for each of the 50 States, and I will make them mandatory if these goals are not met.

I have established an import ceiling for 1980 of 8.2 million barrels a day—well below the level of foreign oil purchases in 1977. I expect our imports to be much lower than this. But the

Appendix C

ceiling will be enforced by an OCI import fee if necessary. I am prepared to lower these imports still further if the other oil-consuming countries will join us in a fair and mutual reduction. If we have a serious shortage, I will not hesitate to impose mandatory gasoline rationing immediately.

The single biggest factor in the inflation rate last year, the increase in the inflation rate last year was from one cause, the skyrocketing prices of OPEC oil. We must take whatever actions are necessary to reduce our dependence on foreign oil—and at the same time reduce inflation.

As individuals and as families, few of us can produce energy by ourselves. But all of us can conserve energy—every one of us, every day of our lives.

Tonight I call on you, in fact all of the people of America, to help our Nation. Conserve energy. Eliminate waste. Make 1980 indeed a year of energy conservation.

Of course, we must take other actions to strengthen our Nation's economy.

First, we will continue to reduce the deficit and then to balance the federal budget.

Second, as we continue to work with business to hold down prices, we will build also on the historic national accord with organized labor to restrain pay increases in a fair fight against inflation.

Third, we will continue our successful efforts to cut paperwork and to dismantle unnecessary government regulation.

Fourth, we will continue our progress in providing jobs for America, concentrating on a major new program to provide training and work for our young people, especially minority youth. It has been said that "a mind is a terrible thing to waste." We will give our young people new hope for jobs and a better life in the 1980s.

And, fifth, we must use the decade of the 1980s to attack the basic structural weaknesses and problems in our economy through measures to increase productivity, savings, and investment.

With these energy and economic policies we will make America even stronger at home in this decade—just as our foreign and defense policies will make us stronger and safer throughout the world.

We will never abandon our struggle for a just and a decent society here at home. That is the heart of America—and it is the source of our ability to inspire other people to defend their own rights abroad.

Our material resources, great as they are, are limited. Our problems are too complex for simple slogans or for quick solutions. We cannot

Appendix C

solve them without effort and sacrifice.

Walter Lippman once reminded us:

"You took the good things for granted. Now you must earn them again. For every right that you cherish, you have a duty which you must fulfill. For every good which you wish to preserve, you will have to sacrifice your comfort and your ease.

"There is nothing for nothing any longer."

Our challenges are formidable. But there is a new spirit of unity and resolve in our country. We move into the 1980s with confidence and hope—and a bright vision of the America we want:

An America strong and free.

An America at peace.

An America with equal rights for all citizens and for women guaranteed in the United States Constitution.

An America with jobs and good health and good education for every citizen.

An America with a clean and bountiful life in our cities and on our farms.

An America that helps to feed the world.

An America secure in filling its own energy needs.

An America of justice, tolerance, and compassion.

THE IRAN CRISIS

For this vision to come true, we must sacrifice, but this national commitment will be an exciting enterprise that will unify our people. Together as one people let us work to build our strength at home, and together as one indivisible union let us seek peace and security throughout the world.

Together let us make of this time of challenge and danger a decade of national resolve and of brave achievement.

Thank you very much.

Jimmy Carter

The White House, *January 23, 1980*.
A Joint Session of the Congress

We will be pleased to provide locations of bookstores in your area selling Logos titles.

Call: (201) 754-0745

Ask for bookstore information service